A Taste of Thailand

RIDER

A Taste of Thailand

DAVID L. SCOTT
AND KRISTIAAN INWOOD

Illustrated by Kristiaan Inwood

Rider

London Melbourne Auckland Johannesburg

Rider & Company
An imprint of the Century Hutchinson Publishing Group
62–65 Chandos Place, Covent Garden, London WC2N 4NW

Century Hutchinson Publishing Group (Australia) Pty Ltd
16–22 Church Street, Hawthorn, Melbourne, Victoria 3122

Century Hutchinson Group (NZ) Ltd
PO Box 40–086, Glenfield, Auckland 10, New Zealand

Century Hutchinson Group SA (Pty) Ltd
PO Box 337, Berglvei, 2012 South Africa

First published 1986

Text © David Scott and Kristiaan Inwood 1986
Illustrations © Kristiaan Inwood 1986

Typeset by Wyvern Typesetting Ltd, Bristol

Printed and bound in Great Britain by
The Guernsey Press Co. Ltd

British Library Cataloguing in Publication Data
Scott, David, *1944-*
A taste of Thailand.
1. Cookery, Thai
I. Title   II. Inwood, Kristiaan
641.59593   TX724.5.T5
ISBN 0–7126–1291–2

Contents

Preface

Oliver Caldecott, editor of Rider Books, suggested this book to David Scott and Kristiaan Inwood and introduced them to one another. The style and content is a synthesis of their complementary talents. Kristiaan lives in Bangkok with his Thai wife, Anong, and their children. He is a writer, graphic designer and illustrator with a considerable knowledge of Thai food and customs. David Scott is a well-known author of foreign and health food cookery books. He has written about Indonesian and Japanese cooking, and knows South-East Asian cuisine well. The result of their combined work is a book of anecdotes and illustrations of Thailand coupled with a sensible practical guide to Thai cooking in a Western kitchen.

A Preamble

I first arrived in Thailand shortly after my twenty-second birthday, and have lived here, approximately half my life, ever since.

Within a week of my arrival I had decided that Thais were delightful, the women the most beautiful (and playful, sensual, feminine, intriguing, etc.) I had ever met, and local food easily the best I had ever tasted.

Nothing has ever changed those opinions.

After three years of hedonistic life I met a lovely, diminutive (4 feet 10¼ inches), delightfully feminine bundle of energy called Anong who, a few years later, became my wife, and mother of three monkeys we co-produced. Now she is the family midget – her offspring tower above her, but she, true to her independent, earthy self, doesn't give a stuff.

Through Anong, I have come to appreciate innumerable aspects of Thailand. Besides being my dictionary, reference library, guide, confidante, wife, lover, major critic, mother of my children, best friend, etc., she is, in my 'umble opinion, the world's best cook of the world's best food.

Her help in my contributions to this book has been of inestimable value.

I hereby acknowledge my prejudices – and gratefully thank her for them.

Kristiaan Inwood
Bangkok, 1985

Cooks' Notes

Although it has been influenced by Indian and Chinese cooking, Thai cuisine is unique. The Thais have absorbed rather than added on other ways of cooking, and they have synthesized their own cohesive, independent style. Their food is hot and spicy and well flavoured with fresh herbs. The appearance of a dish is most important; so much so that vegetable and fruit carving has become a traditional art form, and at a formal meal the visual appeal of the food is as highly regarded as its flavour.

The main religion of Thailand is Buddhism, and in the past the vegetarianism encouraged by this faith has influenced national eating habits. It has not, however, affected the Thai fondness for fish and other seafood, perhaps because they are blessed with an abundant supply of both in their rivers and from the sea. Nowadays meat is more commonly on the menu, but, although compared to Western habits it is still eaten in relatively small amounts, it is probably fair to say that fresh and cooked vegetables, fish, poultry and meat now all play an equal role in the Thai diet. A typical substantial meal will consist of rice plus five or six other dishes. These could include a soup, a fried or steamed dish, a curry, a salad and one or two hot sauces. They are all served at the same time and the diners help themselves in whatever order they choose.

Iced water, hot tea or soft drinks are usually served with meals. Men may also drink iced beer or, more commonly, a local brand of rice whisky. This, mixed liberally with soda, and iced, is regarded as the Thai 'wine' and perfectly complements Thai food. Fresh fruit is served at the end of the meal and, on special occasions, a dessert as well.

Traditionally Thais have eaten with their fingers and a porcelain spoon for soups. Rural folk still eat in this manner but their urban brethren use a spoon and fork and, for certain noodle dishes and Chinese food, chopsticks. A knife is rarely needed since all the ingredients are cut into mouth-size portions before cooking and serving.

The recipes in this book have been carefully selected to give a genuine introduction to Thai cooking. It is, however, very difficult to obtain complete culinary authenticity outside the country of origin, and I decided that wherever a choice had to be made between authenticity and practicality for the Western cook, I would choose the latter. Thus most of the ingredients needed are available in any well-stocked supermarket, and the few unfamiliar ones can be obtained from Oriental or Asian grocery stores. For readers able to obtain those few distinctive Thai ingredients not available in the West, I have named them in the ingredients list alongside the substitute ingredients I have used.

Individuality, creativity and improvisation are the touchstones of a Thai cook, and these qualities describe the spirit you should bring to the recipes given here. All the recipes work well as they are given, but don't be afraid to ad lib if you wish to make dishes that suit your taste perfectly. Thai food approached in this way offers a brand-new culinary experience and an unexplored area of new food ideas and flavours.

You may not be making Thai meals on a regular basis, but the following ingredients are required in many of the recipes and if you have them ready before starting, the book will be much easier to use. Also, once they are in your stock cupboard you may be persuaded to cook Thai dishes more often. Further details of these and other ingredients are given in the Glossary of Ingredients.

Essential Ingredients

Black peppercorns
Chilli peppers, fresh or dried
Coconut flakes or *desiccated coconut*, unsweetened (they are needed to make coconut milk but *frozen, fresh coconut flakes or milk* or *tinned coconut milk* are even handier if they are available)
Coriander, fresh leaves, root and coriander seeds
Fish sauce (available by this name in all Oriental food stores)
Garlic
Ginger root
Lemon juice and *lemon rind* (or *tamarind concentrate* and *lemon grass* if available)
Roasted peanuts or *peanut butter*

Shrimp paste (available in Oriental food stores. *Anchovies* or *anchovy sauce* can be used as a substitute)

Onions

The recipes have been tested using common white or brown onions, and the following approximations have been used:

1 small onion is taken to weigh an average of 2 oz (50 g)
1 medium onion averages 4 oz (100 g)
1 large onion averages 8 oz (225 g)

Shallots are slightly closer in taste to the onions generally used in Thai cooking, and if they are available and you wish to try them in the recipes, substitute 4 shallots for 1 medium-sized onion.

Chicken

To divide a chicken into portions for a curry or for other dishes in which small pieces are required, cut as follows: the leg into 2 pieces; the wing into 2 pieces; the back into 4 pieces; divide the breast down the centre and cut each half into 2 pieces.

Bean curd

A couple of the recipes require bean curd which has been pressed to remove excess moisture. This process makes the bean curd firmer and less likely to break up during cooking. Pressed bean curd may also be fried more easily than the tender, fresh, unpressed curd.

To press bean curd, lay the cakes of bean curd on a wooden cutting board. Place a few sheets of kitchen paper on top and cover them with a plate or flat dish. Weight the dish with a cup of water or a scales weight. Finally tilt the board slightly (rest one end on an upturned saucer) and leave to drain for 1–2 hours. The bean curd is now ready to use.

Garnishes

Thai food is nearly always presented with one or two garnishes to add colour and flavour to the dish. The most popular are finely chopped coriander leaves (or sprigs of coriander) and seeded, finely chopped red or green chillies. Other common garnishes are fried onion flakes (recipe below), thin strips of a thin omelette, chopped spring onions, coarsely crushed roasted peanuts, wedges of lemon or lime, finely chopped cloves of garlic fried golden in vegetable oil, and peeled, halved or quartered boiled eggs. Fresh herbs such as parsley, mint or basil are suitable alternatives if fresh coriander is unavailable and if the garnish is mainly for colour rather than flavour.

Fried onion flakes

Fried onion flakes are used as an all-round garnish. They are most easily made from dried onion rings, but taste best made from fresh onions.

From dried (dehydrated) onion rings   *Serves 4 as a garnish*

4 oz (100 g) dried onion rings
4 fl oz (100 ml) vegetable oil

Heat the oil in a heavy 8 in (20 cm) frying pan. Stir in the onion rings and cook, stirring, until nicely browned. Drain the onions through a sieve and then pat them gently between absorbent sheets of kitchen paper. They are now ready for use. Store unused onion flakes in an airtight jar. They will keep well for up to a week.

From fresh onions   *Serves 4 as a garnish*

2 medium onions, finely sliced
4 fl oz (100 ml) vegetable oil

Press the onion rings between sheets of absorbent kitchen paper to remove the moisture, and then follow the same method as for the dried onion rings.

Equipment

No special equipment is required, but a wok makes some of the stir-frying jobs easier, and a pestle and mortar or electric grinder are very handy for crushing herbs and spice mixtures into a paste.

Quantities and Menus

A formal Thai meal usually consists of rice plus anything from two to six or more dishes. It is therefore difficult in a Western cookery book, when the user may wish to make only one dish at a time, to gauge the quantities to be given in a particular recipe. I have decided to follow the method I have used before and give quantities for about 4 people. Any exceptions to this are indicated in the recipe. Thus you can decide for yourself whether to increase or reduce the quantities given to suit the number of people you are serving and how many dishes you intend to make.

To prepare a menu, select from the recipes one or more vegetable, curry, salad, fish, meat or poultry dishes and serve them with plain rice, a soup and one or two sauces. Finish with fresh fruit and/or a dessert. Remember that in a Thai meal all the dishes are served at the same time and the diners themselves choose in what order and combination they wish to eat them.

Finally, Thai food combines well with other cuisines, so do think about serving a Thai dish as part of a more conventional menu. It will add a little spice and exotica to the meal.

Living to Eat Versus Eating to Live

Broadly speaking, people can be divided into two categories: those who eat to live, and those who live to eat. Thais belong exclusively to the latter category.

The Thai kitchen is the household's social centre where, from dawn to dusk, people congregate to cook, salivate, eat, drink, converse, etc. All Thai households I've known conform in this respect.

Whenever any of Anong's innumerable brothers, sisters, aunts, uncles, nephews, nieces, cousins or family friends stay with us, none stray far from the kitchen. Eating time and siesta time is any time. Certain individuals eat, nap, bathe, clean their teeth (to refresh their palates), eat, nap, bathe, etc. Sometimes, guilt-stricken by idleness, they indulge in the national atonement of ostentatiously guiding a broom through the kitchen, house or garden. It hardly matters if they miss dust or leaves. It's the thought that counts.

Itinerant food vendors perpetually travel the lanes around the house, advertising their wares with distinctive cries. Periodically, our guests emerge from the cool kitchen, blinking like sun-stunned lizards, to ambush them. After purchasing gargantuan snacks, they return kitchenwards by diplomatically circuitous routes.

There *must* be a time when no one is eating. However, like an ant's smile, I've never seen it. The kitchen is relatively empty only when Anong fries peppers. Then bodies flee, sneezing, coughing violently, faces flushed, short of breath, throughout the house and garden. Once the pungent, throat-catching smell dissipates, people furtively return.

Food is inescapable. Throughout Bangkok, vendors ply residential lanes or park outside shopping centres, schools, tourist attractions, markets, factories, hospitals and so on. Makeshift restaurants mushroom in alleys and on vacant ground. Permanent street restaurants range from spartan noodle shops to cavernous establishments offering literally hundreds of Thai and Chinese dishes in every conceivable regional variation.

Food is no less ubiquitous in the countryside. To escape crowds, you might brave a jungle trail towards a remote waterfall. You'll climb hillsides beneath a humid arboreal canopy, scramble over rocks, felled trees and rotting vegetation, negotiate gigantic ferns, creepers and vines, slither down slopes and eventually hear the dull thunder of cascading water. Monkey troops chatter high above. A rainbow cleaves trees. You ache, sweat, but happily approach the rocks lining the waterfall pool, convinced that the odyssey was worthwhile to ensure paradisical solitude. Fat chance. There, awaiting you, is some demure young thing with soft drinks and various snacks.

When the Inwood monkeys were younger, and whenever we visited the beach for a few days, we left Bangkok around sunrise to escape the early morning traffic congestion. Anong would clutter the car with biscuits, bread, buns, tiffin carriers filled with glutinous rice, sausages, salted beef, fried chicken, papaya salads, lettuce, tomatoes, peanuts, chocolates, oranges, grapes and jars of iced water, provisions more suitable for the overland trip to England than to a resort sixty miles away. I often complained, saying we could stop at a restaurant if anyone felt hungry. My wife has always suffered from selective deafness. We'd speed along, Anong and the monkeys busily munching, gurgling, burping. Once replete, they'd sleep until we arrived. Then immediately they awoke they would visit their favourite beachside restaurant for breakfast.

There's a certain logic in all this, since Thai food is undeniably outstanding. The sheer quality and freshness of local seafood, poultry, meats, vegetables, spices and fruits fuel a national culinary talent (Thai men are often excellent cooks, too) to make delicious food. The Thai cuisine embodies the best of Indian and Chinese culinary traditions – noodles, curries, sweet and sour dishes, lengthily cooked and fast-cooked ingredients, exotic spices and condiments – while retaining its own very special character.

Generally, Thai food is chilli hot. Chillies stimulate the appetite and purportedly lower blood pressure. Certainly, it is easy to believe that someone contentedly digesting the choicest part of a ricefield, a school of fish, a herd of cattle, a flock of birds,

a garden and an orchard is serenely placid because his
chilli-reduced blood pressure is at its lowest ebb.

Food ranges from simple rice and noodle dishes to extraordinary exotica – which awakens the sneaking suspicion that
thousands of anonymous martyrs suffered hideous deaths when
sampling various fruits, fungi, berries, crustaceans, reptiles,
spices, herbs, rodents, roots, insects, fish, birds and plants to
discover which were edible.

Food sometimes causes anxiety. Grotesque rumours periodically sweep Thailand claiming that certain foods cause dramatic
shrinkage of male genitalia. Water melons, ducks and Vietnamese noodles have been blamed for this malady.

Food's aphrodisiac properties are a subjective matter. Several
Chinese restaurants offer the male sexual organ of various
animals – including deer, buffalo, tiger, pig, horse and elephant –
fried, grilled, marinated, boiled, baked and broiled in expensive
stews, salads and soups. Enthusiasts (exclusively male) swear
that such dishes rejuvenate the eater. Sceptics remain uncon-
vinced.

Food. What a subject! Food has inspired Thai kings to wax
poetic. Food prompts weekend excursions into the countryside
to visit newly opened restaurants, or far-flung establishments
with secure reputations. Gourmet reminiscences trigger maudlin
sentimentality. Whenever I return from trips abroad or up-
country, Thai friends are infinitely more interested in what I ate
than in where I stayed, what I saw or did, or whom I met. And
food is a, perhaps *the*, national topic of conversation.

The fact is that, at 1 a.m., you can safely assume that any
couple still awake, young or old, mixed, male or female, is
talking about money, food and sex, or food, sex and money, or
sex, money and food . . . .

Exotica

Have you ever enjoyed rice sausages, eaten cucumber, tomato and lettuce salads sprinkled with sugar, or dipped your fresh pineapple in chillied salt?

No?

Probably, you've never lived in Thailand.

Have you ever eaten lotus stems fried with coconuts, added sugar, chillies, grated peanuts and marijuana to your noodles, or eaten grilled field rats?

No?

Probably, you've never lived in Thailand.

Have you ever eaten Crab Darling, fried tree ants or locusts, or aubergine and frog curries?

No?

Probably, you've never lived in Thailand.

Have you ever eaten cobra meat, elephant's penis soup or spicy jellyfish salads?

No?

You haven't missed much.

Decency forbids mention of the most exotic fare which appears to have been inspired either by the common Oriental male preoccupation/phobia/dread of age and impotency, or the need for revitalization after a heavy night. (The most extraordinary breakfast/pick-me-up I ever saw was a mixture of raw duck eggs, iced lemonade and chillies which was swallowed and immediately followed by a tumblerful of neat whisky!)

David Scott has considerately avoided any heavy stuff.

Dear reader, you don't realize how lucky you are. . . .

Glossary of Ingredients

Below is some detailed information on the basic ingredients of Thai cooking, which includes methods of using and preparing them and, where appropriate, information on substitute ingredients.

Chillies

Many varieties of chilli pepper are grown in Thailand but for the purposes of this book they are the serrano type (2–4 in/5–10 cm long, ¼ in/1 cm thick) which are most commonly available in the West. Three types are usually on sale: the green, immature chilli, the red, mature chilli and the dried red variety. If you are cutting fresh chillies it is best to wear rubber gloves as they can irritate the skin. Do not touch your eyes with the gloves, and wash the gloves immediately the job is finished. To reduce the fierceness of chilli peppers remove the seeds. Alternatively, leave the chillies to soak in cold water for an hour before adding them to the dish. You can also add them whole to the dish when cooking, and remove them before serving.

Dried chillies are as hot as the fresh variety, but because they contain no volatile oils they do not burn the skin as quickly. Red and green chillies are equally hot, though there is no method of predicting the strength of a particular chilli, and even within the same batch some are hotter than others.

One teaspoon of hot pepper sauce used as a substitute for fresh or dried chillies is equivalent to 2 medium fresh or dried chilli peppers. Chinese-style hot pepper sauce, not the Mexican variety, has been used in the recipes that contain chilli sauce. The Thais also have their own distinctive hot sauce, called *Nam Prik*. It is flavoured with salted fish and lime juice as well as chilli peppers. A recipe is given in the chapter on Sauces.

Note: Hotness is a hallmark of Thai food, but the degree of 'fire' is up to the individual cook. If you or your guests are unused to hot food, be careful about the amount of chilli pepper you use. Since chillies vary so much in strength always err initially on the side of caution when deciding how much to put in.

Chinese dried black mushrooms

These mushrooms have a different flavour from that of the mushrooms we normally use in the West. They are readily available in Chinese grocery stores, and their use in Thai cooking reflects the Chinese origins of some Thai dishes. The mushrooms are always sold dried, and before use they need soaking for 30 minutes in hot water. The stems are tough and inedible and must be cut off after the soaking period.

Coconut milk

This is not the liquid inside a coconut, which is called coconut water, but the liquid pressed from grated coconut flesh diluted with water or from dried coconut after it has been soaked in hot water or milk or a mixture of both. In Thailand, coconut milk would normally be made from fresh coconut flesh. It is an important flavouring and thickening agent, and is also used to make soup stocks. Strictly speaking, there are three grades of coconut milk used in cooking. The category depends on whether the milk has been obtained from unpressed (thick), once pressed (medium) or twice pressed (thin) grated coconut flesh.

South-East Asian cooking uses coconut milk in a number of recipes and especially in curries. This often puts off potential cooks in the West, who think it is unavailable. This is not so. Coconut milk is easily made from the dried, unsweetened coconut flakes or desiccated coconut available in health and wholefood stores. It is also available tinned, and a quick substitute can be made from cow's milk mixed with coconut extract or essence, or by simply dissolving creamed coconut in hot water. Coconut cream, if called for, can be spooned off from the top of refrigerated thick coconut milk; alternatively, sour cream is a good substitute. Methods 1–4 below explain the various ways of making coconut milk. Method 1 makes authentic coconut milk and method 4 is a convenient but only just fair substitute. Methods 2 and 3 are in between. Tinned coconut milk, if available, is the easiest way of obtaining a good-quality substitute for the newly made, fresh coconut variety.

The recipes in this book that use coconut milk normally call for the all-purpose, medium-thickness variety. The recipes below show how to prepare this and also give variations for preparing thin or thick coconut milks.

NB: All methods yield 12 fl oz (350 ml)

Method 1: Coconut Milk from Fresh Coconut

5 oz (150 g) grated fresh coconut *or* frozen grated coconut, defrosted
12 fl oz (350 ml) hot water

Put the coconut and water into a blender and process at low speed for 5 minutes. Line a sieve with cheesecloth or a dampened, clean tea towel and pour in the coconut mixture. Let it drain through for 5 minutes and then press the residue with the back of a wooden spoon to extract the last of the milk. The liquid collected is the all-purpose coconut milk used in many of the recipes in this book.

For a thin coconut milk, repeat the process using the coconut residue left in the sieve in place of the fresh coconut.

For a thick coconut milk, follow method 1 but use 7 oz (200 g) grated fresh or frozen coconut. Store coconut milk in the refrigerator. It has the same shelf life as ordinary milk.

Method 2: Coconut Milk from Dried Unsweetened Coconut

2 oz (50 g) dried unsweetened coconut flakes *or* desiccated coconut
8 fl oz (225 ml) cows' milk
8 fl oz (225 ml) water

Put the coconut, milk and water into a pan and bring almost to the boil. Stir occasionally. Leave the mixture to cool slightly and then blend it for a minute or two. Line a sieve with cheesecloth or a dampened, clean tea towel and pour through it the contents of the blender. Let it drain through for 5 minutes, and then press the residue with the back of a wooden spoon to extract the last of the milk. The liquid collected is the all-purpose coconut milk used in many of the recipes in this book.

For a thin coconut milk, repeat the above process using the coconut residue left in the sieve and use water in place of milk.

For a thick coconut milk, follow method 2 but use all milk rather than half milk and half water.

Method 3: Coconut Milk from Creamed Coconut

4 oz (100 g) creamed coconut
12 fl oz (350 g) hot water

Blend the coconut cream in the hot water and strain the mixture through a sieve lined with cheesecloth or a dampened, clean tea towel. This method makes medium-thickness, all-purpose coconut milk.

For thicker or thinner milks use 1 oz (25 g) more or less creamed coconut.

Method 4: Instant Coconut Milk

12 fl oz (350 ml) cows' milk
1 teaspoon coconut extract *or* essence

Stir the extract into the milk. It is now ready for use. For thick coconut milk use half single cream and half milk. For thin coconut milk use half milk and half water.

Storing coconut milk: Coconut milk freezes very well, and it is a good idea to make more than you need and freeze the rest. Pour the milk into small plastic bags or containers, seal them and freeze. Defrost at room temperature, or submerge the plastic bag or container in hot water. A microwave oven could also be used.

Coconut cream from coconut milk: Put the coconut milk made by method 1 or 2 (thick milk variations) into a glass container in the refrigerator and leave it to rest for 30 minutes to 1 hour. The coconut cream will rise to the top, where it can be spooned off. Coconut cream is sometimes used in curries and desserts. The amount obtained depends on the quality of the coconut or, if you have used the dried coconut method, the quality of the cows' milk and the oil content of the dried coconut.

Tinned coconut milk: This is generally available from Chinese or Indian grocery stores. Use the unsweetened variety, and stir it before use. The quality is as good as that of coconut milk made from dried coconut or from the so-called fresh coconuts available in the West.

Coriander

Also well known as Chinese parsley (and to a lesser extent, cilantro), coriander is an essential ingredient in Thai cooking. The leaves are used in flavouring and decoration, the crushed seeds in curries and other spiced dishes and, unique to Thai cuisine, the roots, crushed to a paste with garlic and black pepper, are used in a variety of marinades and sauces.

For flavouring purposes fresh coriander leaves may be replaced by the dried herb, and for garnishes fresh parsley, basil or mint may be substituted. Fresh coriander roots can be found on the stems of bunches of fresh coriander, although in the West the natural long, trailing roots have usually been cut short. However, by cutting off all the available roots plus a little of the stems, enough can normally be collected to proceed with a recipe. Having said that, we are aware that a recipe requiring coriander roots may seem to a Western cook too obscure to tackle and we have included this ingredient only in a few recipes very basic to Thai cooking.

Fish sauce (Nam Pla)

Fish sauce is to Thai cooking what soya sauce is to the Japanese and Chinese cuisines. It is made from the liquid extracted from salted, fermented shrimps and fish. Fish sauce can be bought by that name from Chinese grocery stores. It is thin in consistency and quite salty. Where it is used in a recipe, extra salt is rarely necessary.

If fish sauce is unavailable, make a substitute by grinding or blending 2 anchovy fillets with 1 clove of garlic, 2 tablespoons (30 ml) of water and 1 tablespoon (15 ml) of soya sauce.

Galangal (Laos in Indonesian, Ka in Thai)

A member of the ginger family, galangal is sold in the West only in its powdered form. It has a flavour somewhere between pepper and ginger.

Ginger

Many types of ginger are grown in Thailand for culinary, medicinal and ornamental purposes. Freshly picked young ginger is used in cooking when it is in season, but otherwise the Thais use stored ginger root which is essentially the same as the kind we buy in the West and call fresh ginger. If you are buying ginger look for plump roots with a smooth, shiny, unwrinkled skin. Before use, peel off the skin and finely chop or grate the flesh. Ground ginger powder should not be used as a substitute for fresh ginger except in an emergency. Pickled, crystallized or preserved ginger sometimes makes a fair substitute.

Lemon grass

This is what gives Thai dishes that familiar, characteristic flavour and smell of lemon. Fresh lemon grass is not normally available in the West, and in the recipes given here grated lemon rind is used as a substitute. You may of course use the fresh plant if available, or the dried or powdered varieties. Dried stems of lemon grass need soaking in hot water before use. The powdered kind is added straight to the cooking pot.

Noodles

Many varieties are used in Thai cooking, but in the recipes here only three types are used.

Rice sticks, also called *rice vermicelli*, are very thin, brittle, dried rice flour noodles. They can be deep-fried straight from the packet, as in the Thai dish *mee krob*, or treated as ordinary noodles.

Egg noodles are the regular egg and wheat flour noodles sold in Chinese grocery stores. They are cooked by boiling in water; after boiling and draining they can additionally be shallow- or deep-fried. Occasionally fresh egg noodles are available in Oriental stores, sometimes in the deep-freeze section.

Cellophane noodles or *bean threads* are made from mung bean flour. They are a thin, brittle noodle but after soaking in hot water become soft, slippery to the touch and semi-transparent. They expand a lot on soaking and 4 oz (100 g) is usually enough for a meal for 4 people.

Shrimp paste (Kapee or Blachan)

This is a pungent paste made from dried shrimps. It is sold dried in slabs and is available in Chinese and Asian grocery stores. Store it in an airtight container. The fish odour of the paste disappears during cooking, but on opening the container the smell is strong and it is a good idea to leave the kitchen windows open or to put on the extractor fan. Anchovy paste, mashed anchovies, bottled prawn or shrimp sauce or even anchovy-flavoured soya sauce may be used as substitutes.

Shrimp paste is a common ingredient in Thai cooking, but in the recipes given here I have been careful in its use since it is an acquired taste to Westerners.

Tamarind

The tamarind tree produces a fruit pod whose sour juices are used as a flavouring agent in Thai cooking. The pods are sold pressed into a pulp which is soaked in water and then filtered through a sieve. The brown liquid collected is called tamarind water. It is used in curries, soups, stews, sauces etc. An easy way to prepare tamarind water in the West is to use the tamarind concentrate available from Indian grocery stores. The concentrate is diluted as required (1 teaspoon to 3 tablespoons water). Alternatively, lemon juice or lime juice sweetened with a little dark brown sugar may be used as a substitute. In the recipes given here tamarind water and lemon or lime juice are used in the same proportions if the latter are used as substitutes.

Thai Fire

Chillies (*Capsicum*) are vital ingredients of the best Thai food. On an ascending scale (from, say, 'Strewth!' to 'Jesus Christ!'), there are three major varieties of chillies used in Thai cooking.

The mildest, *Capsicum grossum*, bell pepper in English, and *Prik On* or *Prik Nuom* in Thai ('weak or young pepper'), is relatively painless, some 2 inches long and usually a pale green. Bell peppers are used in mild sweet and sour dishes and relatively bland condiments for noodles and so on.

Capsicum frutescens, spur peppers in English, and *Prik Chee Fah* in Thai (or 'pointing skywards peppers', after the way they grow) are either red or green and are also some 2 inches long. The red variety is hotter than the green, the dried variety hotter than the fresh. Both, with their seeds removed, are eminently chewable fresh, pickled, grilled or boiled. Spur peppers are also used in sweet and sour dishes, in mild condiments, and to enliven various fried dishes.

The hottest (deadliest, most blasphemous, etc.) is *Capsicum minimum* (something of a joke), guinea pepper in English, and in Thai *Prik Kee Noo*, or (a *very* polite translation this) 'rat droppings peppers' after their approximately ¾ inch lengths and suggestive shapes. Guinea peppers, usually a lustrous green – and a very bright red when ripe – are used whole or sliced in condiments, Thai salads and piquant soups. They are *exclusively* responsible for the hottest 'fire' in the finest Thai food.

All chillies are undeniably popular. But whether for culinary, or other, reasons one can merely surmise. Enthusiasts claim several properties, such as cleansing the blood and lowering high blood pressure; reducing cholesterol; protecting against colds, malaria, extreme elements; developing physical strength; and stimulating burgeoning romantic inclinations.

You pays your money, you takes your choice.

Soups

Chicken stock•Vegetable stock•Chicken and mushroom soup•
Pork and bamboo shoot soup•Hot and sour prawn soup•Quick
hot and sour beef soup•Noodle and Chinese cabbage soup•
Noodle and pork soup•Fish ball and mushroom soup•
Mushroom soup•Cabbage soup•Lemon, chicken and coconut
milk soup

A Thai meal nearly always includes a soup; even at breakfast a thin rice soup may be served. *Gwaytio Nam*, a substantial noodle soup, is popular as a quick midday snack or light meal; busy office workers buy it from one of the many roadside food stalls which specialize in this dish. The soup is made with chicken or beef stock and includes thin slices of pork or small fish balls. It is topped with coriander leaves, chopped spring onions and, believe it or not, whole fresh chilli peppers. Optional extras include more chillies, ground peanuts, fried garlic flakes and fish sauce (*Nam Pla*), which Thais add to almost everything.

Soup served for the evening meal is made from a clear or very thin stock and it is served at the same time as the other dishes. The soup is presented in a tureen, or sometimes, in a restaurant, in a Mongolian soup pot. This device, nicknamed the fire pot, has a central funnel of hot fiery coals that keep the soup very hot throughout the meal.

Chicken Stock   *Makes 5 pints (2.8 litres)*

Chicken stock is required for several of the soup recipes and for other dishes in this book. For convenience and speed you may wish to use stock cubes, but for a really good chicken stock to provide the basis for an excellent soup or sauce, use the following recipe.

3 lb (1.4 kg) stewing chicken, quartered, *or* the same weight in chicken parts
6 pints (3.3 litres) water
1 large onion, quartered
4 celery tops
6 peppercorns
½ in (2.5 cm) piece of ginger root, peeled
2 teaspoons (10 ml) soya sauce

Put the chicken pieces into a large pot and add the water, onion, celery tops, peppercorns and ginger root. Bring to the boil, reduce heat, cover and simmer for 1½ hours. Remove the chicken (the chicken meat may be used in other dishes). Strain the soup and return it to the pan. Add the soya sauce and simmer for a further 5 minutes. If the stock is required immediately, skim off the fat; otherwise let it cool and then refrigerate it. Excess solidified fat may now be removed easily from the surface of the stock.

Vegetable Stock   *Makes 2 pints (1.1 litres)*

This stock is suitable for use in the soup recipes and other dishes in this book. Its flavour is mild, but it will nevertheless change subtly depending on which selection of vegetables you use.

1½ lb (700 g) of three or more of the following vegetables: broccoli, bean sprouts, cabbage, carrots, celery, courgettes, cauliflower, green beans, leeks, onions, pea pods, spring onions, turnips, watercress (including stems)
3 pints (1.7 litres) water
8 oz (225 g) mushrooms and stalks, sliced, *or* just stalks may be used
1 teaspoon salt
2 teaspoons (10 ml) light soya sauce
½ teaspoon sugar

Combine the vegetables and water in a large saucepan. Add the mushrooms and salt and bring to the boil. Reduce heat, cover and simmer for 45 minutes. Strain the stock through a fine sieve and return it to the pan. Boil it down to 2 pints (1.1 litres) and then stir in the soya sauce and sugar. It is now ready to use.

Variation
Replace the fresh mushrooms with 8 dried Chinese mushrooms. After straining off the used vegetables pick out the mushrooms, discard the stems and use the mushroom caps in other recipes.

Chicken and Mushroom Soup

This is a delicious soup using the characteristic Thai combination of garlic, peppercorns and coriander for flavouring. Method 1 is simple, quick and uses easily obtainable ingredients. Method 2 is the authentic Thai way of preparing the soup. It is particularly tasty but takes longer to prepare than Method 1 and may involve more effort in obtaining the ingredients.

Method 1   *Serves 4–6*

1 tablespoon (15 ml) vegetable oil
2 cloves garlic, crushed
1 teaspoon coriander seeds, ground
5 black peppercorns, ground
8 oz (225 g) cooked chicken meat, finely chopped
2 pints (1.1 litres) chicken stock
1 tablespoon (15 ml) fish sauce *or* light soya sauce
salt if needed
4 oz (100 g) mushrooms, thinly sliced

Garnish
2 spring onions, cut into 1 in (2.5 cm) strips

Heat the oil in a saucepan and add the garlic and ground coriander and peppercorns. Stir over a moderate heat for about half a minute and then add the chicken. Stir over the heat for a minute and then slowly pour in the chicken stock. Add the fish or soya sauce, stir well and taste. Add salt if needed. Bring to the boil, reduce the heat, cover the pan and simmer for 15 minutes. Add the mushrooms and simmer for a further 5 minutes. Adjust the seasoning and serve garnished with spring onions.

Method 2   *Serves 8*

2 lb (900 g) uncooked chicken, cleaned
6 spring onions, chopped
1 teaspoon salt
4 pints (2.3 litres) water
5 dried Chinese mushrooms
3 cloves garlic, crushed
8 black peppercorns, ground
1 tablespoon chopped coriander root
1 tablespoon (15 ml) vegetable oil
1 tablespoon (15 ml) fish sauce

Put the chicken whole into a large saucepan and add half the spring onions, salt and water. Bring to the boil, reduce heat, cover and simmer for 2 hours or until the chicken is tender. During this time soak the Chinese mushrooms in hot water for 30 minutes, then cut off the stems and cut the mushrooms in half. Now lift the chicken out of the pan and strain off the stock. Put it on one side. Cut all the chicken flesh from the bones, cut it into small pieces and set it aside. In a mortar, grind the garlic, peppercorns and coriander roots into a paste. Heat the oil over a moderate heat and fry the paste, stirring, for 1 minute. Add the chicken meat and cook and stir for another minute. Add the stock and fish sauce and bring to the boil. Add the Chinese mushrooms, reduce the heat and simmer for a couple of minutes. Serve the soup garnished with the remaining spring onions, finely chopped.

Pork and Bamboo Shoot Soup *Serves 4*

This northern Thai soup works well with tinned bamboo shoots and is thus well suited to the Western kitchen. For a thick soup including eggs, see the variation below.

2 tablespoons (30 ml) vegetable oil
1 clove garlic, crushed
½ teaspoon coriander seed, ground
¼ teaspoon freshly ground black pepper
8 oz (225 g) raw, lean pork, thinly sliced
1 tablespoon (15 ml) fish sauce *or* soya sauce
2 teaspoons white sugar
2 pints (1.1 litres) stock, chicken *or* meat
12 oz (350 g) tinned bamboo shoots, drained and thinly sliced

Garnish
finely chopped spring onions *or* watercress

Heat the oil in a large saucepan and stir in the garlic, coriander and black pepper. Fry until the garlic is just lightly browned. Stir in the pork and sauté the meat until browned on both sides. Add the fish sauce, sugar and stock and bring to the boil. Reduce the heat, cover and simmer for 15 minutes. Add the bamboo shoots, stir well, return to the boil, adjust the seasoning and serve garnished with a light sprinkling of spring onions or watercress.

Variation

For a more substantial soup, add to the finished soup over a
moderate heat, 2 oz (50 g) cooked shrimps. Heat them through
and then pour slowly into the soup through a sieve, stirring, two
beaten eggs. Serve immediately.

Hot and Sour Prawn Soup *Serves 4*

This is a very sour and very hot soup. The authentic version is
probably too fiery for the unsuspecting and I have reduced the
amount of chilli peppers that would traditionally be used in
Thailand. Add more if you wish. For a simple version of this
soup follow the prawn variation given after the quick hot and
sour beef soup recipe below.

1 tablespoon (15 ml) vegetable oil
1 lb (450 g) fresh prawns, shelled but with the heads reserved
2 pints (1.1 litres) stock *or* water
1 teaspoon grated lemon rind *or* 1 stalk lemon grass cut into 1 in
    (2.5 cm) lengths
1 fresh *or* dried green chilli, thinly sliced
salt to taste
2 teaspoons (10 ml) fish sauce *or* light soya sauce
2 tablespoons (30 ml) fresh lemon *or* lime juice

Garnish
½–1 fresh *or* dried red chilli, seeded and thinly sliced
freshly chopped coriander leaves

Heat the oil in a large saucepan and add the prawn heads. Stir-fry
for 3–4 minutes and then add the stock, lemon rind, chilli and salt
to taste. Bring to the boil, reduce the heat, cover and simmer for
15 minutes. Strain the mixture through a fine sieve and return the
stock to the pan. Bring to the boil and add the prawns, then
reduce the heat and cook until the prawns are tender but still firm
(about 3 minutes). Remove from the heat, stir in the fish sauce
and lemon juice. Pour the soup into a tureen, sprinkle the chillies
and coriander leaves over the top, and serve immediately.

Quick Hot and Sour Beef Soup *Serves 4*

The recipe I have given for this spicy, sharp soup has been slightly
Westernized but it is speedy and simple to prepare and similar
enough to the authentic dish to be delicious.

1 tablespoon (15 ml) vegetable oil
2 cloves garlic, crushed
½ teaspoon coriander seeds, ground
¾ teaspoon freshly ground black pepper
8 oz (225 g) lean beef cut into thin strips about
    ½ in/1 cm by 1½ in/4 cm
2 pints (1.1 litres) stock
2 bay leaves
1 teaspoon grated lemon rind
1 tablespoon (15 ml) fresh lemon juice
1 teaspoon (5 ml) fish sauce *or* soya sauce
¼ teaspoon (1.25 ml) hot pepper sauce
salt to taste

Garnish
4 oz (100 g) bean sprouts, washed and drained

Heat the oil in a large saucepan and add the garlic, coriander and black pepper. Stir the mixture until the garlic is just browning. Add the meat and brown on both sides. Add the remaining ingredients, stir well and bring to the boil. Reduce the heat, cover and simmer for 1 hour or until the beef is tender. Adjust the seasoning and serve garnished with a sprinkling of bean sprouts over each bowl.

Variations

For a quick hot and sour prawn soup replace the beef with 1 lb (450 g) prawns, shelled, and then follow the method above. Fresh fish stock is best for this variation, but you can use stock cubes if you wish.

Noodle and Chinese Cabbage Soup   *Serves 4–6*

This is a vegetable version of a popular Thai soup. For a meat variation see the recipe below. This soup tastes just as good with rice noodles or other types of noodle.

6 oz (175 g) dried egg noodles
1 tablespoon (15 ml) vegetable oil
3 cloves garlic, crushed
2 pints (1.1 litres) vegetable stock *or* chicken stock
8 oz (225 g) Chinese cabbage, thinly sliced
soya sauce to taste
4 oz (100 g) bean sprouts

Garnish
1 tablespoon coriander leaves, chopped
2 oz (50 g) roasted peanuts, coarsely crushed
1–2 fresh *or* dried red chillies, seeded and finely chopped
½–1 tablespoon white sugar

Cook the noodles in plenty of boiling water, according to the instructions on the packet, or until just tender. Drain and rinse under cold water until cooled to room temperature. Set them aside. Heat the oil in a large saucepan and sauté the garlic golden. Add the stock and bring to the boil. Put in the cabbage and simmer for 2 minutes. Add soya sauce to taste. Stir in the bean sprouts and noodles and simmer until the noodles are heated through. Pour the soup into a tureen and sprinkle over the top the coriander leaves, peanuts, chilli peppers and sugar. Serve immediately.

Noodle and Pork Soup

Follow the recipe above but brown minced pork 2 oz (50 g) with the garlic. Replace the soya sauce with fish sauce and stir into the soup, with the noodles, 8 oz (225 g) lean cooked pork, thinly sliced.

Fish Ball and Mushroom Soup   *Serves 4–6*

Ready-made fish balls can be purchased in Oriental food stores, but instructions for their preparation at home, if you have the time, are given in the recipe. Fish ball soup is a popular street or snack food in Thailand, where the locals find it very handy and tasty for a quick lunch.

Fish balls
8 oz (225 g) white fish, no bones and no skin included
  in the weight
1 teaspoon coriander seeds, ground
3 cloves garlic, crushed
½ teaspoon freshly ground black pepper
¼ teaspoon salt
1 egg white, beaten just stiff

Soup
1 tablespoon (15 ml) vegetable oil
2 pints (1.1 litres) chicken stock
5 Chinese mushrooms, soaked in
  hot water, stems removed
2 tablespoons (30 ml) fish sauce *or*
  soya sauce
2 spring onions, finely chopped
freshly ground black pepper to taste

Garnish
3 tablespoons finely chopped
  coriander leaves and stems

To make the fish balls, put the fish flesh, coriander, 1 clove garlic,
pepper and salt into a blender (or use a pestle and mortar) and
grind to a paste. Scrape the paste into a bowl and stir in the egg
white. Form the mixture into small, marble-sized balls and set
them aside.

Heat the oil in a large saucepan and sauté the remaining garlic
golden. Add the stock and bring to the boil. Add the
mushrooms, reduce the heat and simmer for 5 minutes. Put in the
fish balls carefully and return the soup to a gentle simmer. Leave
to cook until the fish balls float to the top. Stir in the fish sauce and
add black pepper to taste. Remove the pan from the heat. Stir in
the spring onions. Serve garnished with chopped coriander.

Variation

For a more filling soup add 8 oz (225 g) bean curd, cubed, at the
same time as the fish balls.

Mushroom Soup *Serves 4*

This soup and the cabbage soup below are simple peasant dishes. They are quick to make and tasty if you have a good stock available.

1 tablespoon (15 ml) vegetable oil
2 cloves garlic, crushed
½ teaspoon coriander seeds, ground
¼ teaspoon freshly ground black pepper
2 teaspoons (10 ml) fish sauce *or* soya sauce
2 pints (1.1 litres) vegetable stock *or* chicken stock
4 medium-sized mushrooms, wiped and thinly sliced

Garnish

2 spring onions, finely chopped
1 tablespoon finely chopped coriander leaves
1 fresh *or* dried red chilli, seeded and thinly sliced (optional)

Heat the oil in a large saucepan and stir in the garlic, coriander and black pepper. Fry with stirring until the garlic just turns golden. Add the fish sauce and stock and bring to a low simmer. Simmer for 10 minutes, then add the mushrooms. Simmer for a further 5 minutes and then serve the soup garnished with chopped spring onions, coriander leaves and, if you like hot food, chilli pepper rings as well.

Variation

Replace the mushrooms with 4 dried Chinese mushrooms soaked in hot water for 30 minutes, drained, stems removed and discarded and the caps sliced.

Cabbage Soup

Follow the mushroom soup recipe but replace the mushrooms with 10 oz (300 g) cabbage or Chinese cabbage, thinly sliced. After adding the cabbage simmer for 6–7 minutes or until the cabbage is just tender.

Lemon, Chicken and Coconut Milk Soup *Serves 4*

A lemon-flavoured soup, creamy in texture because of the coconut milk. The recipe is versatile, and thinly sliced beef or small, firm pieces of white fish may be substituted for the chicken.

1 pint (550 ml) water
1 pint (550 ml) coconut milk (see page *19*)
2 chicken breasts *or* legs and thighs, chopped into bite-sized
  pieces (leave the bones in or debone before cutting up,
  whichever you choose)
2 teaspoons grated lemon rind *or* 3 stalks lemon grass, chopped
2 spring onions, finely chopped
1–2 fresh *or* dried red chillies, seeded and finely sliced
juice of 1 lemon *or* lime
2 tablespoons (30 ml) fish sauce *or* soya sauce

Garnish
1 tablespoon finely chopped coriander leaves

Combine the water and coconut milk in a large saucepan and bring to a slow boil. Add the chicken pieces and lemon rind. Reduce the heat and simmer uncovered (if the pot is covered the coconut milk may curdle) for 15–20 minutes, or until the chicken is tender. Add the spring onions and chillies. Stir in the lemon juice and fish sauce and serve immediately, garnished with coriander leaves.

Creep Orf the Grass

There are two major grasses (three, if you include marijuana) used in traditional Thai cuisine.

The strongest comes in many varieties, can grow to over a hundred feet tall, is used to build bridges and rafts, to fashion musical instruments, baskets and paper; is a major ingredient at a young and literally tender age in spicy salads, stews and curries; can be eaten as a slightly bitter vegetable; is naturally white but appears as a crunchy yellow after boiling; and is universally known as bamboo.

The second, lemon grass, is used in spicy soups, curries and salads to enhance fragrance; is largely tasteless; is traditionally believed to relieve intestinal wind when used in food; and is customarily boiled with water which, after cooling, is used by Thai and Chinese women who have just given birth for a refreshing, cleansing and fragrant bath.

And Mary Jane is used by villagers, either mixed with chillies and fish sauce to make a condiment, or sprinkled liberally into salads and curries exclusively to stimulate the appetite.

Other stimulation is *purely* coincidental.

Starters or Side Dishes

Prawn salad with dressing•Galloping horses•Green
apples with sweet hot sauce•Stuffed Chinese mushrooms
with sweet and sour sauce•Spiced beef with mint leaves•
Celery and green peppers with sesame sauce•Plump horses•
Son-in-law eggs•Spring rolls•Fried broccoli and prawns•Sautéed
crab meat and greens•

Starters as such are not common in a Thai meal since more often
than not all the dishes are served at once or brought to the table as
soon as they are prepared. However, I have selected the
following recipes as suitable starters for a Western-style meal.
They make unusual and exotic dishes to begin any meal, or they
can be served as side dishes and, in some cases, as main courses in
a conventional Thai dinner.

Prawn Salad with Dressing   *Serves 4*

This is a simple starter. It looks delicious served on sparkling white plates.

Salad

8 oz (225 g) cooked prawns
2 in (5 cm) cucumber, unpeeled, seeded and finely sliced
1 small green pepper, seeded and finely sliced
1 tomato, diced
1 small onion, *or* half a Spanish onion, finely sliced

Dressing

1 tablespoon (15 ml) cider *or* rice wine vinegar
2 tablespoons (30 ml) fish sauce
3 tablespoons (45 ml) lemon juice
¼ teaspoon (1.25 ml) chilli sauce
¼ teaspoon white sugar

Garnish

2 spring onions, finely sliced

Place all the salad ingredients in a large bowl. Combine the dressing ingredients and mix well. Pour the dressing over the salad and toss. Chill. When you are ready to serve the salad, drain it well and divide it among 4 small white plates. Garnish with spring onion rings.

Galloping Horses   *Serves 6–8*

I am not sure why this dish is called galloping horses, but its name inspires the imagination to try it. Fresh pineapple is required in the recipe, but if it is not available see the variation below which uses oranges instead.

3 tablespoons (45 ml) vegetable oil (peanut oil is good)
3 tablespoons finely diced onion
1 lb (450 g) minced lean pork
1 teaspoon salt
½ teaspoon freshly ground black pepper
1 tablespoon sugar
2 oz (50 g) roasted unsalted peanuts, coarsely crushed,
  or crunchy peanut butter

1 medium to large fresh pineapple, peeled, sliced and
the hard centre removed

Garnish
1 red chilli, seeded and finely chopped
fresh coriander or mint leaves, finely chopped

Heat the oil in a frying pan and sauté the onion for 1 minute. Add
the pork, salt, black pepper and sugar, stir well and cook over a
moderate heat, stirring often, for 10–15 minutes. Stir in the
peanuts and remove from the heat. Arrange the pineapple slices
on individual plates and spoon a portion of the pork mixture into
each. Garnish with a few rings of chilli pepper and a sprinkling of
coriander or mint leaves.

Variation
Arrange on lettuce leaves, on individual plates, segments from 3
or 4 large oranges. Spoon the pork mixture over, garnish as
above and serve.

Green Apples with Sweet Hot Sauce   *Serves 4*

In Thailand this dish would be made with green mangoes, and if
they are available substitute them for the apples. Otherwise use
crisp, only slightly sweet apples, such as Granny Smiths. Serving
apples in this way usually causes a surprise – people are not used
to seeing them in such strange company.

4 crisp green apples, cored and sliced into six
1 teaspoon (5 ml) lemon juice
3 tablespoons (45 ml) fish sauce
4 oz (100 g) white sugar
¼–½ teaspoon (1.25–2.5 ml) chilli sauce
1 tablespoon finely diced onion

Place the apple pieces in a bowl of water to which the lemon juice
has been added, and put them in the fridge to chill slightly (15–30
minutes). Put the fish sauce and sugar in a small pan and gently
melt the sugar in the liquid. Pour the mixture into a small bowl
and set it aside for 10 minutes to cool. Now stir in the chilli sauce
and onion. Set the bowl of sauce in the centre of a plate, arrange
the apple slices around it, and serve.

Stuffed Chinese Mushrooms
with Sweet and Sour Sauce   *Serves 4*

Rehydrated Chinese black mushrooms have large caps which are
perfect for stuffing. This recipe also requires bamboo shoots.
Buy a very small tin, store unused shoots under clear water, and
use within 3–4 days.

8 Chinese black mushrooms
5 oz (125 g) minced pork
1 tablespoon finely chopped bamboo shoots
2 spring onions, finely chopped
1 teaspoon finely chopped coriander leaves
2 tablespoons (30 ml) soya sauce
2 teaspoons (10 ml) cider vinegar *or* rice wine vinegar
2 tablespoons (30 ml) vegetable oil (peanut oil is good)
2 tablespoons (30 ml) chicken stock *or* other stock
1 teaspoon cornflour
¼ teaspoon salt
1 teaspoon sugar

Garnish

coriander leaves, finely chopped
1 red chilli, seeded and finely chopped (optional)

Cover the mushrooms in warm water and leave to soak for 30
minutes. Drain well, then remove and discard the hard, inedible
stalks. Combine the pork, bamboo shoots, spring onions,
coriander leaves, half the soya sauce and half the vinegar. Stir this
mixture well and fill each of the mushroom caps with it. Put the
caps in a steamer (or between 2 plates standing on a bowl in a pan
with water in the bottom), and steam for 20 minutes. Just before
they are finished put the oil, stock, cornflour, salt, sugar and
remaining soya sauce and vinegar in a small pan and heat,
stirring, until just boiling, Serve the mushrooms with this hot
sauce poured over and garnished with coriander leaves. Top with
a few rings of chilli if desired.

Spiced Beef with Mint Leaves   *Serves 4*

Serve this spicy beef dish with sticks of raw vegetables, like
French *crudités*, and use them to scoop up the beef mixture.

12 oz (350 g) minced lean beef
3 cloves garlic
2 tablespoons finely diced onion
¼–½ teaspoon (1.25–2.5 ml) chilli sauce
1 teaspoon coriander seeds, crushed
juice of 1 lemon
1 tablespoon (15 ml) fish sauce
1 spring onion, chopped (optional)

Garnish
finely chopped mint

Accompaniment
raw vegetable sticks, e.g. celery, green pepper, carrots,
chicory leaves

In a non-stick or heavy frying pan carefully sear the beef, without
oil, until it is just lightly browned. Turn it into a bowl and leave
to cool to room temperature. Wrap the garlic and onion together
in a piece of aluminium foil and heat the foil parcel in a dry frying
pan for 1 minute. Turn the garlic and onion into a blender and add
the chilli sauce, crushed coriander seeds, lemon juice, fish sauce
and spring onion. Blend it to a thick sauce or paste. Stir the sauce
into the beef and turn the mixture out onto a serving plate.
Garnish with chopped mint and serve with a bowl of attractively
cut raw vegetables.

Celery and Green Peppers with Sesame Sauce　*Serves 4*

This is a light, tasty, Chinese-inspired dish.

2–3 sticks celery including leaves, washed
1 large green pepper
1 tablespoon (15 ml) sesame seed oil
2 tablespoons (30 ml) soya sauce
1 teaspoon brown sugar

Garnish

8 very thin slivers of peeled fresh ginger root
2 teaspoons sesame seeds, dry roasted

Cut the celery diagonally into 2 in (5 cm) lengths. Retain the leaves for use in the garnish. Cut the pepper in half, core and seed, cut in half again and then cut each piece into quarters. Boil a pan of slightly salted water and blanch the celery and pepper pieces for 30 seconds only. Remove and drain. Mix together the oil, soya sauce and brown sugar. Stir this sauce into the vegetables and distribute them among 4 individual plates. Garnish each with a few chopped celery leaves, slivers of ginger root and sesame seeds.

Variation

For a sweet and sour sauce add 1 tablespoon (15 ml) lemon juice to the sauce ingredients.

Plump Horses　　　　　　　　　　　*Serves 4*

I think the name of this dish must relate to the poached egg shape of the individual portions. Anyway, it's a good talking point for the guests while they enjoy the taste.

4 eggs, beaten
4 oz (100 g) minced chicken *or* pork *or* beef, *or* a mixture of two
　of them
8 fl oz (225 ml) stock
2 cloves garlic, crushed
1 teaspoon coriander seeds, ground
1–2 spring onions, finely chopped
salt and freshly ground black pepper to taste

Garnish

finely chopped coriander *or* mint *or* parsley

Combine all the ingredients except the garnish and mix well. Distribute the mixture among 4 (or 8 if they are not large enough) individual poached egg moulds. Set them in an egg poacher with the water 1 in (2.5 cm) or so up the sides of the moulds. Cover and cook over a low heat until they are set (about 20 minutes). Serve them hot, still in the moulds, garnished with the finely chopped herbs.

Son-in-law Eggs   *Serves 4*

This is another one of those recipes with an inspired name. The story goes that a prospective bridegroom wanted to impress his future mother-in-law with his culinary prowess. He devised this recipe from the only other dish he could make, boiled eggs. It is delicious and I am sure he won her over, at least for a while.

4 eggs, hard-boiled, shelled and cut in half crosswise
oil for deep-frying
2 tablespoons brown sugar
2 tablespoons (30 ml) fish sauce
2 tablespoons (30 ml) lemon juice *or* tamarind water

Garnish
2 tablespoons diced onion, fried brown in a little oil
2 tablespoons finely chopped coriander leaves
1–2 red chillies, seeded and thinly sliced

Heat the oil in a wok or deep-fryer with a basket until it is just beginning to smoke, and then carefully lower in the boiled egg halves. Deep-fry them for 3–4 minutes. Remove, and set aside to drain. Heat 1 tablespoon (15 ml) of oil in a saucepan and stir in the fish sauce, lemon juice and sugar. Simmer over a very low heat, stirring, for 5 minutes. Add the eggs and stir them very gently over the heat for 2–3 minutes. With a slotted spoon transfer the eggs to a serving plate. Garnish them with fried onion, coriander leaves and rings of chilli.

Spring Rolls *Serves 6*

Spring rolls are as popular in Thai cuisine as they are in Chinese. This recipe has been slightly Westernized to suit the availability of particular ingredients, but the spring rolls are nevertheless delicious and very popular with almost everybody.

The pancakes for making spring rolls are quite easy to make but you can, if you wish, buy them ready-made in any relatively well-stocked Chinese grocery store. The pancakes, or spring-roll skins as they are known to the Chinese, are thin and made from an egg-rich batter. The filling given here is vegetable-based and contains no meat or fish. If you wish to add prawns, chicken or pork, which would be more authentically Thai, follow the variation below the main recipe. Spring rolls may also be served as a main course.

Batter

5 oz (150 g) plain flour, sifted
1 oz (25 g) cornflour
4 eggs
15 fl oz (450 ml) water
vegetable oil for shallow frying
or 12–15 ready-made spring-roll skins

Filling

vegetable oil for shallow- and deep-frying
1 green pepper, seeded and thinly sliced
2 sticks celery, finely chopped *or* 4 oz (100 g) bamboo shoots, finely chopped
2 spring onions
1 clove garlic, crushed
1 teaspoon peeled, grated ginger root
6 oz (175 g) mushrooms, sliced
12 oz (350 g) bean sprouts, washed and drained
2 tablespoons (30 ml) fish sauce *or* soya sauce
2 fl oz (50 ml) water

Garnish

finely chopped mint leaves (optional)

Combine the batter ingredients, except the oil, in a mixing bowl or electric blender and beat into a smooth batter. Brush the bottom of an 8 in (20 cm) frying pan with a thin coating of oil and heat it over a medium flame. Pour in enough batter to cover the bottom of the pan very thinly. As soon as the bottom side starts to brown turn the pancake over and just cook the other side. Remove the pancake from the pan and repeat the procedure until almost all the batter is used up (about 12 pancakes). Reserve a little of the batter (about 2 tablespoons/30 ml) for later use. Stack the cooked pancakes one on top of the other.

To make the filling, heat 1 tablespoon (15 ml) oil in a large frying pan or wok and over a medium flame stir-fry the green pepper and celery for 2 minutes. Add the spring onions, garlic and ginger and stir-fry for 1 minute. Add the mushrooms and bean sprouts and stir-fry for 1 minute. Add the soya sauce and water and continue stir-frying until the bean sprouts are well wilted. Remove the pan from the heat.

Divide the filling among the spring roll skins. Spoon the filling onto each one and roll it up, tucking in the edges as you go. Seal the flap with a little of the reserved batter thickened with a little flour. Deep-fry the filled spring rolls in deep, hot vegetable oil (peanut oil is traditionally used) until crisp and golden brown. Drain and serve right away, garnished with mint leaves.

Variation
Replace the bean sprouts in the filling ingredients with a mixture of 4 oz (100 g) bean sprouts, 4 oz (100 g) cooked, shredded pork and 4 oz (100 g) cooked, shredded chicken meat or cooked small prawns. Follow the main recipe, adding the substituted mixture where the bean sprouts would have been added, and making sure the pork and chicken are browned during frying.

Fried Broccoli and Prawns   *Serves 4–6*

Serve as a starter or side dish, or with rice as a main course.

1 lb (450 g) broccoli, cut into bite-sized pieces
2 tablespoons (30 ml) vegetable oil
4 cloves garlic, crushed
1 tablespoon (15 ml) fish sauce *or* soya sauce
8 oz (225 g) cooked prawns

Put the broccoli in a bowl of iced water for 10–15 minutes. Heat the oil in a frying pan or wok and fry the garlic golden. Drain the broccoli and toss it into the pan or wok. Stir-fry for 2 minutes, reduce the heat, cover the pan and leave to simmer over a very low heat for 5 minutes. The broccoli should be just tender but still retain some crunch. Stir in the fish sauce and prawns, heat through and serve.

Sautéed Crab Meat and Greens *Serves 4*

For the greens in this recipe use whatever is in season, such as
spinach, spring cabbage, lettuce or Chinese cabbage (Peking or
Baak Choi or *Choi Sum*). With tinned crab meat this dish is quick
to make and excellent as a starter or side dish.

2 tablespoons (30 ml) vegetable oil
4–6 cloves garlic, crushed
6 oz (175 g) cooked crab meat, shredded
1 lb (450 g) fresh greens, washed, drained and very coarsely
  chopped
2 tablespoons (30 ml) fish sauce *or* soya sauce
freshly ground black pepper to taste

Heat the oil in a wok or heavy frying pan and fry the garlic
golden. Add the crab meat and stir-fry until very hot. Drop in the
greens and stir-fry until the leaves start to wilt. Sprinkle in the
fish sauce and black pepper to taste, and turn the heat down low.
Cover the pan or wok and simmer for 3–4 minutes or until the
greens are tender. Serve immediately.

Pedigree Grain

The Thai expression for 'eat', *Kin Khao*, literally means 'eat rice'.
Other Thai expressions approximating 'eat' evoke 'gobble rice',
'savour rice' and 'scoff rice'. More than 35 million of Thailand's
some 50 million people spend their lives cultivating rice, easily
the most important Thai crop. Rice is the principal food for
humans and animals; it inspires festive celebrations and influences
Buddhist monasticism's annual regimen. It provides major
government revenue, and for centuries has been Thailand's
leading export.

Rice is income, rice is fuel, rice is sustenance, rice is security,
rice is fun, rice is versatility, rice has a mother, rice has a soul, rice
is meat and potatoes and bread and butter and very nearly
ambrosia to the Thais – to whom a riceless meal is almost a
travesty.

Rice can be naturally red, purple, brown, blackish, yellow or
off-white. Red or brown rice – not polished white, therefore not
'beautiful' and accordingly reserved for dogs, convicts and
neurotic health food freaks – is largely that from which the husk
has been removed, leaving nourishing bran layers and germ on
the grain.

Rice comes in several varieties with short, medium or long
grains. There is, Anong's youngest farming brother informs me,
wild and swamp-growing rice, lowland rice, upland rice,
mountain rice, dwarf rice, floating rice, rice that favours deep
water and rice that grows very much taller than Thai men.

Rice powers a potent liquor that swiftly induces newtlike
behaviour (I write from experience). Rice can be transformed
into an almost infinite variety of sweets, cakes, biscuits, desserts
and noodles. Rice can be fluffy, gooey, glutinous, crisp, hard and
chewy, served as a porridge or as a soup. Rice can be fried, boiled,
stewed, baked or grilled, and is vastly more versatile than
potatoes or bread.

Similar versatility extends to by-products that have numerous industrial uses. Rice, in various guises (I read) is found in polishes, fertilizers, livestock and poultry feeds, vitamin supplements, soap, even beer.

Thailand's annual rice-planting season officially begins with Bangkok's Royal Ploughing Ceremony each April or May, when solemn Brahmanic rites symbolize the attention that the Hindu divinities Vishnu and Indra give to the new season.

Around the same time, and with substantially less solemnity, villagers in the north-east fire gigantic and decidedly phallic home-made rockets heavenwards to 'ensure' bountiful rains during the forthcoming rice-planting season. Attendant celebrations are boisterous and ribald (the festival does, after all, concern fertility), and the occasion affords participants the last real chance for letting off steam before arduous, earnest field work begins.

Two or three months later, Buddhist monks vow to forego travel and remain overnight in their monasteries during the annual three-month Rains Retreat. This tradition predates Buddhism. In ancient India, all mendicants and itinerant sages spent these three months in a fixed abode for fear of accidentally trampling young rice plants which, during the season of exuberant growth, would have detrimentally affected the alms-giving peasantry.

Deference of another kind is shown to Mae Phosop, the Rice Mother spirit who becomes pregnant when rice flowers bloom. She, like many pregnant women, entertains unusual tastes. These are addressed, in the area from which Anong hails, by ritual offerings of rice liquor, boiled eggs, bitter fruits, rice gruel, burning incense and floral garlands placed beneath shade-giving trees edging village ricefields.

Similar reverence is shown to Mae Phosop's offspring, the crop, which has a soul. After harvesting, a mere handful of rice is ritually stored in an appropriately high, and therefore auspicious, place in the farmer's granary. This handful contains the crop's soul and is eventually mixed with seeds to impregnate the farmer's next crop. This continuity recalls the lovely Buddhist simile for rebirth in which one candle flame is lighted from another. The new flame is not the same as the old, yet neither is it different.

Rice-related tales could fill an entire book. Yet the important thing is that the Thai invitation to 'eat rice' ('savour rice', 'scoff rice', etc.) is commonly an introduction to companionship, friendship, to a dining experience where, with everyone taking food from communal dishes, an extra diner can easily be accommodated and provided with his own rice – the grain whose religious, mythological, ritual, mystical, magical connections give it the most exotic pedigree imaginable.

Rice & Noodles

Plain boiled rice•Plain fried rice•Combination fried
rice•Vegetarian fried rice•Thai fried noodles•Chicken and
broccoli fried rice•Bean curd and broccoli fried rice•Pineapple
fried rice•Rice stuffed pineapple•Fried noodles and bean
Curd•Egg noodles, meat and broccoli•Noodles with
combination topping•Fried bean noodles•Thai fried crisp
noodles•Vegetarian fried crisp noodles

The Thais, like most of the peoples of South-East Asia, like their
rice white and polished. Long- and short-grain (also called
glutinous or sticky) rice are the two types used, although within
these categories there are many different grades of quality. As the
staple accompaniment to all meals in southern Thailand they use
long-grain rice, and in the north short grain. All over Thailand
short-grain rice is used in the preparation of sweet dishes such as
rice boiled in thick coconut milk and served with ripe mangoes,
one of the most popular and most delicious of Thai desserts.

Noodles are an important feature of Thai cuisine. They are
used in many different shapes and forms but fall into four main
categories: egg noodles, rice vermicelli (or rice sticks), rice
noodles which are the only noodles packaged wet, and mung-
bean noodles (also called cellophane noodles). Egg noodles,
made from wheat flour, eggs and water, are probably the most
familiar, and those usually encountered in Chinese restaurants.
They are served boiled, stir-fried and in soups. Rice vermicelli
made from rice flour are normally soaked before use and then
used in stir-fried dishes or soups. However, in the famous Thai
dish *Mee Krob* they are deep-fried straight from the packet. They
puff up to twice their size during frying and are then served
mixed with meat, vegetables and a sweet and sour sauce. Mung-
bean noodles, like rice noodles, are first soaked and then used in
stir-fried dishes or soups, or they are deep-fried straight from the

packet. They have a neutral flavour and tend to soak up the flavours of the other ingredients they are cooked with. Rice noodles are used straight from the packet, cut into whatever lengths you require. They are served plain boiled with a sauce, or stir-fried, or in soups. See the Glossary of Ingredients for more information on noodles.

Plain Boiled Rice   *Serves 4–6*

The following instructions are for loose rice. If you buy packaged rice, follow the instructions given on the packet. Note that no salt or oil are used.

Long-grain rice
1 lb (450 g) rice
1¾ pints (1 litre) water

Short-grain rice
1 lb (450 g) rice
1¼ pints (700 ml) water

Wash the rice in lots of running cold water, moving the rice around with your fingers. Once the water stops running milky, set the rice aside to drain. Measure the cooking water into a pan and add the rice. Bring to the boil over a high heat. Reduce the heat, cover the pot with a tight-fitting lid and simmer for 20 minutes. Remove the pan from the heat, take off the lid, fluff up the rice with a wooden spoon and serve.

Plain Fried Rice   *Serves 4*

3 tablespoons (45 ml) vegetable oil
2 cloves garlic, finely chopped
1 medium onion, finely chopped
1 red *or* green pepper, seeded and chopped
1 in (2.5 cm) piece ginger root, peeled and cut into fine slivers
   (optional)
2 tablespoons fish sauce *or* soya sauce
1¼ lb (550 g) cooked rice
2 tablespoons (30 ml) tomato purée

Garnish

1 small *or* ½ medium cucumber, sliced
2 tablespoons chopped coriander leaves

Heat the oil in a wok or large saucepan. Add the garlic and onion
and fry until the onion is softened. Add the pepper and ginger, if
used, and stir-fry for 2 minutes. Add the fish sauce, stir well and
then add the rice and tomato purée. Stir-fry until the rice is well
heated through. Transfer to a serving dish and surround with a
ring of cucumber slices. Garnish the rice with coriander leaves
and serve immediately.

Variation 1

Replace the green pepper with 8 oz (225 g) cooked prawns or
shrimps.

Variation 2

For a more substantial dish add to the frying onion 8 oz (225 g)
lean pork, cubed, or 8 oz (225 g) bean curd, pressed and cubed.

Combination Fried Rice   *Serves 4–6*

Combination fried rice is useful as a one-dish meal, or it can be
served as part of a more elaborate dinner-party menu.

2 fl oz (50 ml) vegetable oil
2 medium onions, finely chopped
2 cloves garlic, finely chopped
1–2 red chillies, seeded and finely chopped
8 oz (225 g) lean pork, cut into thin strips
3 eggs, lightly beaten

1½ lb (700 g) cooked rice
2 tablespoons (30 ml) fish sauce
3 tablespoons tomato ketchup (tomato ketchup is a
   popular ingredient in Thai cookery. Use tomato purée
   if you prefer)
8 oz (225 g) cooked small prawns *or* shredded cooked
   chicken *or* slices of Chinese salami sausage
1 teaspoon salt

Garnish

4 spring onions, chopped
2 tablespoons chopped coriander leaves
1 lemon *or* lime cut into wedges

Heat the oil in a wok or large saucepan. Add the onions, garlic
and chilli and fry until the onion is softened. Add the pork and
stir-fry until it is just cooked (about 3 minutes). Pour the eggs
into the middle of this mixture and stir-fry until they are well
combined. Stir in the rice, fish sauce, tomato ketchup, prawns
and salt. Stir-fry until the rice is heated through and all the
ingredients are well mixed (about 5 minutes). Transfer to a large
plate or bowl, garnish with spring onions, coriander leaves and
lemon wedges and serve at once.

Variation

Cut a 1 in (2.5 cm) piece of ginger root into fine slices, and fry
with the onions, garlic and chilli.

Vegetarian Fried Rice   *Serves 4–6*

Follow the recipe for Combination fried rice (above), but
substitute for the pork 3 oz (75 g) bean sprouts, 1 green pepper,
seeded and finely chopped, and 2 tomatoes, finely chopped.
Replace the fish sauce with soya sauce. Leave out the prawns.

Thai Fried Noodles　　　　　　　　　　*Serves 4*

Thin rice noodles are soaked, drained, stir-fried with shrimps and flavoured with tomato, lemon, garlic and fish sauce. This is not a chilli hot dish, but chilli sauce could be added if you wish.

12 oz (350 g) rice vermicelli
4 fl oz (100 ml) vegetable oil
2 cloves garlic, finely chopped
1 medium onion, finely chopped
8 oz (225 g) cooked shrimps *or* small prawns
2 tablespoons tomato ketchup *or* tomato purée
2 teaspoons sugar
1 tablespoon (15 ml) fish sauce
2 tablespoons (30 ml) lemon juice *or* tamarind water
2 eggs, beaten
4 oz (100 g) bean sprouts
2 tablespoons peanuts, coarsely ground *or* crunchy peanut butter

Garnish

2 tablespoons chopped coriander leaves
1 lemon, cut into wedges
1 red chilli, seeded and thinly sliced (optional)

Put the rice vermicelli into a large bowl and just cover with very hot water, then set aside for 10 minutes. Drain, rinse with cold water and set aside. Heat the oil in a large wok or saucepan and add the garlic and onion. Stir-fry until the onion softens. Add the shrimps and heat through. Stir in the tomato ketchup, sugar, fish sauce and lemon juice. Pour in the beaten eggs, give them 2–3 minutes and then stir into the mixture. Add the noodles, half of the bean sprouts and peanuts, mix well and toss and stir until the noodles are heated through. Turn onto a serving dish. Place the remaining bean sprouts on one side of the noodles and then garnish the dish with coriander leaves, lemon wedges and chilli peppers (if used). Serve immediately.

Variation

Replace the rice noodles with cooked egg noodles.

Chicken and Broccoli Fried Rice　　　　　*Serves 4*

3 tablespoons (45 ml) vegetable oil
2 cloves garlic, finely chopped

½ chicken breast, cut into thin strips about 1–2 in (2.5–5 cm) long
8 oz (225 g) broccoli, cut into bite-size pieces
2 tablespoons (30 ml) fish sauce
½ teaspoon chilli sauce, optional
1¼ lb (550 g) cooked rice

Garnish

1 egg, beaten, fried as a thin omelette and cut into strips
2 tablespoons chopped coriander
1 tomato, cut into wedges
1 lemon, cut into wedges

Heat the oil in a wok or large saucepan, add the garlic and fry golden. Add the chicken and stir-fry for 2 minutes. Add the broccoli and stir-fry a further 2 minutes. Stir in the fish sauce and chilli sauce and then the rice. Stir-fry until the rice is well heated through. Transfer to a large serving plate or bowl. Decorate the top with strips of omelette, and garnish with coriander and wedges of tomato and lemon.

Variation 1

For a chilli hot dish add to the frying garlic 2–4 fresh chillies, seeded and finely chopped. Omit the chilli sauce later.

Variation 2

For a curried dish, substitute 1 teaspoon curry powder for the chilli sauce.

Bean Curd and Broccoli Fried Rice   *Serves 4*

In the recipe above, substitute for the chicken 6 oz (175 g) bean curd, drained and cut into ½ in (1 cm) cubes. For a completely vegetarian dish replace the fish sauce by soya sauce.

Pineapple Fried Rice   *Serves 4*

2 fl oz (50 ml) vegetable oil
1 green chilli, seeded and finely chopped
1 medium onion *or* 3 shallots, finely chopped
8 oz (225 g) lean pork diced in ¾ in (2 cm) cubes
4 oz (100 g) cooked small prawns *or* cooked crab meat, shredded
1¼ lb (550 g) cooked rice
2 tablespoons (30 ml) fish sauce *or* soya sauce
8 oz (225 g) tinned *or* fresh pineapple, diced

Garnish
sprig of parsley *or* mint

Heat the oil in a wok or large saucepan and fry the chilli and onion
until the onion is softened. Add the pork and brown on all sides.
Stir in the prawns and heat through. Toss into the pan the rice and
fish sauce and stir-fry for 3–4 minutes. Add the pineapple and
stir-fry for a further 2 minutes. Serve immediately, garnished
with sprigs of mint or parsley.

Rice-Stuffed Pineapple   *Serves 4*

Cut the top off a large pineapple about a quarter of the way down.
Scoop out all the flesh. Cut it into cubes and use 8 oz (225 g) to
prepare Pineapple fried rice (above). Pre-heat the oven to 350° F
(180°C, gas mark 4). Stuff the hollowed-out pineapple with the
fried rice, put the top back on and bake for 15 minutes.

Fried Noodles and Bean Curd   *Serves 4*

Replace the shrimps in the Pineapple Fried Rice recipe with 8 oz
(225 g) bean curd, drained, pressed and cut into ½ in (1 cm) cubes.
Follow the recipe, browning the bean curd at the frying stage.

Egg Noodles, Meat and Broccoli   *Serves 4*

Serve this dish on its own with rice for a lunch dish. It may also be
served as part of a larger main meal.

8 oz (225 g) egg noodles
8 oz (225 g) lean pork *or* beef, cut into thin strips ½ in (1.25 cm)
    by 1 in (2.5 cm)
8 fl oz (225 ml) stock
3 tablespoons (45 ml) vegetable oil
2 cloves garlic, finely chopped
8 oz (225 g) broccoli, cut into mouth-size pieces
2 tablespoons (30 ml) fish sauce
2 tablespoons (30 ml) oyster sauce if available
salt and black pepper to taste

Cook the egg noodles in plenty of boiling water until they are just
tender. Immediately drain and rinse under cold water until they
are cooled. Set aside. Simmer the meat in the stock until just
tender. Heat the oil in a wok or large saucepan and fry the garlic

golden. Add the broccoli and stir-fry for 2 minutes. Add the noodles, toss and fry for 2 minutes. Put in the meat and stock, fish sauce, oyster sauce and salt and black pepper to taste. Mix well, heat through and serve immediately.

Noodles with Combination Topping   *Serves 4–6*

In this dish the noodles are cooked separately and then served topped with a stir-fried mixture of pork, prawns and Chinese mushrooms. It's very quick to prepare once the ingredients are marshalled together.

1 lb (450 g) rice noodles *or* 8 oz (225 g) egg noodles
4 tablespoons (60 ml) vegetable oil
2 cloves garlic, finely chopped
8 oz (225 g) lean pork cut into thin strips ½ in (1.25 cm) by 1 in (2.5 cm)
8 oz (225 g) cooked prawns *or* shrimps
6 spring onions, finely chopped
6 dried Chinese mushrooms, soaked in hot water for 30 minutes, drained, stems discarded and the caps sliced
2 tablespoons (30 ml) fish sauce

Garnish
1 tablespoon chopped coriander leaves

Cook the noodles in plenty of salted boiling water until just tender (about 5 minutes for the rice noodles, 10–12 minutes for the egg noodles). Drain immediately and rinse in cold water until cooled to room temperature. Set aside. Heat the oil in a wok or large saucepan and add the garlic and pork. Stir-fry for 2–3 minutes. Add the prawns or shrimps and heat through. Stir in the spring onions, mushroom slices and fish sauce and stir-fry for 2 minutes. Pour boiling water over the noodles, drain them and transfer to a warmed serving dish. Pour the pork mixture over, then garnish with coriander leaves and serve.

Fried Bean Noodles   *Serves 4*

Bean noodles are made from a purée of mung beans and water, strained and then dried into sheets before pressing into noodles. They are hard and rubbery before soaking, but afterwards become soft and semi-transparent. In this recipe the noodles are soaked and then stir-fried with shrimps, chicken and vegetables.

8 oz (225 g) mung bean noodles
3 tablespoons (45 ml) vegetable oil
3 cloves garlic, finely chopped
4 oz (100 g) cooked shrimps *or* small prawns
4 oz (100 g) cooked chicken, cut into thin slices
2 eggs
2 sticks celery, including leaves, finely chopped
2 spring onions, finely chopped
4 oz (100 g) bean sprouts
1 tablespoon (15 ml) fish sauce
1 teaspoon freshly ground black pepper

Garnish
2 oz (50 g) roasted peanuts, coarsely ground
coriander leaves

Soak the noodles in hot water for 3–4 minutes. Drain and cut
them into 4 in (10 cm) lengths. Heat the oil in a wok or large
frying pan and add the garlic. Fry golden and then add the
shrimps and chicken. Heat through and stir in the noodles, then
make a hole in the centre, break in the eggs and slowly stir them
until just set. Now stir in the celery, spring onions and bean
sprouts. Stir in the fish sauce and black pepper. Transfer to a
serving dish, sprinkle the ground peanuts and coriander over the
dish and serve.

Thai Fried Crisp Noodles   *Serves 4–6*

This dish, called *Mee Krob*, is a Thai speciality. Very fine rice
noodles are first fried until crisp and then stir-fried with a
combination of pork, shrimps, chicken, bean curd and eggs in a
sweet and sour sauce. Chinese rice sticks may be substituted for
very thin rice vermicelli if it is unavailable.

6 oz (175 g) rice vermicelli
vegetable oil for deep-frying
1 medium onion, finely chopped
3 cloves garlic, finely chopped
1–2 red chillies, seeded and finely chopped (optional)
6 oz (175 g) pork fillet, cut into strips
1 chicken breast, skinned, boned and cut into strips *or* use
    cooked chicken meat
4 oz (100 g) cooked *or* raw small shrimps
2 teaspoons grated lemon peel

2 tablespoons (30 ml) soya sauce
2 tablespoons (30 ml) rice vinegar *or* cider vinegar
2 tablespoons (30 ml) lemon juice
2 tablespoons sugar
4 eggs, beaten

Garnish

4 oz (100 g) bean sprouts
chopped coriander leaves

Heat the oil in a wok or deep frying pan and carefully drop in small handfuls of the rice vermicelli (rice vermicelli is very brittle and flies everywhere when broken. It is easier to break it into small pieces inside a large plastic bag.) Fry them for just about half a minute and then turn them over and fry until golden brown and crisp. Remove them with a slotted spoon and repeat for all the noodles. Set them aside to drain on absorbent kitchen paper. Pour the oil out of the wok or frying pan, leaving about 4 tablespoons behind. Fry the onion, garlic and chillies (if used) until softened, then add the pork and lightly brown it. Add the chicken and stir-fry for 3–4 minutes. Stir in the shrimps and reduce the heat to very low. In a bowl combine the lemon peel, soya sauce, vinegar, lemon juice and sugar. Add this mixture to the wok or pan and continue to simmer for a few minutes. Turn the heat up and make a hole in the middle of the ingredients and pour in the eggs. Leave to set a little, and then stir into the other ingredients until well set. Add the fried noodles and toss the mixture well to distribute all the ingredients equally. Turn onto a serving dish, scatter bean sprouts over the top, garnish with coriander leaves and serve.

Vegetarian Fried Crisp Noodles   *Serves 4–6*

As above but replace the pork and chicken with 8 oz (225 g) drained, pressed bean curd cut into 1 in (2.5 cm) cubes, and 6 Chinese mushrooms, soaked for 30 minutes in hot water, stems discarded and the caps sliced. Follow the recipe but omit the shrimps.

Salad Daze

Thai salads are in a class of their own. Almost all are fiery and exceptionally delicious. Preparing the most popular, the classic *Som Tam* – best made with unripe papaya, although cucumbers, marrows and carrots are adequate substitutes – is a sensually pleasurable activity that makes Thai women second happiest.

Preparing the commonest form of *Som Tam* requires one green papaya, sugar, lemons, tomatoes, garlic, guinea peppers, dried shrimps, peanuts, fish sauce, one razor-sharp machete, one plate, one large pestle and mortar, one adventurous Thai female (the rule rather than the exception) and ten or fifteen minutes.

The papaya is peeled, washed and then lightly, repeatedly, hit lengthwise with the machete blade. Thin slices, uneven, irregular, from one- to three-sixteenths of an inch wide and thick, and some three to four inches long, accumulate. The irregularity of the slices contributes to the salad's subtlety. Uniform slices made by grating render the salad's texture dull and uninteresting.

The next step is to place five to eight guinea peppers, uncut, unsliced, in the mortar with some raw garlic. The mixture is vigorously pounded and mashed. Peanuts and dried shrimps are added, and then sliced tomatoes, sugar, two tablespoons of fish sauce and the juice of half a lemon. The ingredients are then pounded and blended. Frequent samplings are made, and necessary additions – more lemon juice to increase tartness, more sugar for sweetness, etc. – advance the mixture to the preferred potency. Finally, the sliced papaya is added.

The entire mixture is stirred and lightly pounded to marry its diverse tastes and textures. This is the most delicate part of the operation. Too heavy a pounding makes the papaya limp and unappetizing. Too light a beating does not sufficiently blend the flavours. The ideal *Som Tam* is one in which the papaya is softened on the outside but remains crisp inside, with each flavour and texture immediately identifiable.

The real beauty of *Som Tam* is that its ingredients are never precisely measured, and no two salads ever taste the same. And besides the standard recipe given here, there are several variations. Tiny ricefield crabs are popular substitutes for shrimps and peanuts, and fermented fish often complements traditional ingredients.

Som Tam can be eaten for breakfast, lunch, dinner or supper, makes an excellent snack, can be enjoyed by itself or eaten wrapped in fresh lettuce or raw cabbage leaves, and is particularly enjoyable with glutinous rice and freshly grilled chicken.

And which sensually pleasurable activities make Thai women happiest?

Eating *Som Tam*.

And doing it twice a day.

Salads & Pickles

Pickled mixed vegetables•Pickled chilli peppers•Cucumber relish•Cucumber salad•Cooked vegetable salad in coconut sauce• Beef and chilli salad•Pork and green apple salad•Pork and cabbage salad•Grapefruit and coconut salad•Prawn, watercress and peanut salad•Fiery fish salad•Cucumber boats with beef cargo•Big salad•Vegetable salad with hot sauce

Thai salads or *Yams* are usually a mixture of one or more of fresh or cooked vegetables, fruit, meat, fish or chicken, served in a variety of combinations in a hot and/or fish sauce or dressing. They are served with rice and other dishes, although some of them are suitable as a main-course salad in the Western manner. Salads are usually garnished with coriander leaves and sliced red chillies. Approach most of the salads given here with caution if you are unused to hot food, and reduce the chilli content to your taste.

Pickled Mixed Vegetables   *Makes 3 pints (1.7 litres)*

Pickled vegetables in the Thai manner may be served as soon as they are made and still warm, or from the refrigerator where, stored in an airtight jar, they will keep for up to two weeks. Serve them with fried fish, chicken or meat dishes. A variety of vegetables are suitable for pickling – select from those suggested a combination that suits availability and your own tastes.

1 pint (550 ml) cider vinegar *or* rice vinegar
1 tablespoon white sugar
1 teaspoon salt
1 lb (450 g) total weight of one of the following vegetables, or a combination:
cauliflower cut into bite-sized pieces
cabbage (white *or* spring, chopped into 1½ in (4 cm) squares)
Chinese cabbage, including *Baak Choi* and Peking, chopped into 1½ in (4 cm) squares

cucumber, peeled, seeded and cut into bite-size pieces
carrots, peeled and cut into bite-size pieces
broccoli, cut into bite-size pieces
green beans, cut into bite-size pieces
corn kernels, cut fresh from the cob
celery, cut into bite-size pieces
6 cloves garlic, finely chopped
6 red chillis (use fewer for a less fiery pickle), seeded and finely
    chopped
6 shallots *or* 1 onion, finely diced
6 fl oz (175 ml) peanut oil *or* sesame oil

Garnish

1 oz (25 g) sesame seeds, dry roasted light brown

Heat the vinegar, sugar and salt in a large saucepan and cook the
chosen vegetables in the mixture individually. Remove them just
before they are tender so that some 'bite' remains in the texture.
Set them aside.
    In a food blender or with a pestle and mortar grind the garlic,
chillies and shallots into a paste. Add a little of the oil if the paste is
too thick to remove from the blender goblet. Heat the remaining
oil in a wok or frying pan and fry the paste, stirring, for 2 or 3
minutes. Add the vegetables and stir-fry over a high heat for 30
seconds. Pour the contents of the wok or frying pan into a serving
dish and sprinkle with toasted sesame seeds if serving immediately. Alternatively, allow to cool and store in clean glass screw-top
jars in the refrigerator.

Pickled Chilli Peppers   *Makes ½ pint (275 ml)*

Pickled chillies are useful for adding a little fire to mildly
flavoured dishes. They keep well and make a colourful alternative
to dried chillies and/or chilli sauce for seasoning and garnishing.

6 fresh red chillies, seeded and thinly sliced
4 tablespoons (60 ml) rice vinegar *or* cider vinegar
4 fl oz (100 ml) water
¼ teaspoon salt
½ teaspoon white sugar

Combine all the ingredients in a clean glass jar. Store in the
refrigerator and use as required. The chillies will keep for up to a
month.

Cucumber Relish   *Serves 4–6*

Cucumber relish is delicious with cold chicken, meat or fish
dishes. In the West it goes well with cheese and it provides a spicy
counterpoint to a mild-flavoured cheese.

1 medium cucumber, peeled, halved lengthwise, seeded and
    coarsely grated
1 tablespoon finely diced onion
1–2 fresh red chillies (less if you want a less fiery relish), seeded
    and finely chopped
1 teaspoon sugar
1 tablespoon (15 ml) lemon *or* lime juice
1 tablespoon (15 ml) fish sauce *or* soya sauce

Mix all the ingredients together in a bowl and serve immediately.

Cucumber Salad   *Serves 4*

1 medium cucumber, peeled, halved lengthwise, seeded and
    finely sliced
2 tablespoons finely diced onion
1 tablespoon finely chopped spring onion
juice of 1 lemon
1 tablespoon (15 ml) soya sauce
1 teaspoon sugar
¼ teaspoon (1.25 ml) chilli sauce (optional)
¼ teaspoon freshly ground black pepper

Combine the cucumber, onion and spring onion in a serving
bowl. Mix together the lemon juice, soya sauce, sugar, chilli sauce
(if used) and black pepper. Pour this dressing over the cucumber
salad. Toss well and serve.

Cooked Vegetable Salad in Coconut Sauce   *Serves 6*

Thai vegetable salad is a cooked, spicy vegetable dish served hot
with rice and other dishes. The vegetables are cooked in coconut
milk until just tender, and then mixed with a hot, lemon-
flavoured paste. Any convenient combination from the selection
of vegetables suggested may be used.

1½ lb (700 g) total weight of a combination of 3 or more of the
    following:

aubergines, cut into 2 in (5 cm) cubes
French beans, cut into 2 in (5 cm) lengths
cauliflower, cut into bite-size florets
Chinese cabbage (including *Baak Choi, Choy Sum* or Peking) cut
   into 2 in (5 cm) strips
green peppers, seeded, cut into 1 in (2.5 cm) strips
carrots, peeled and cut into rounds
broccoli, cut into bite-size pieces
turnips, cut into bite-size pieces

16 fl oz (450 ml) coconut milk (see page 19)
salt to taste
2 oz (50 g) creamed coconut
2 fl oz (50 ml) water
2 tablespoons finely chopped onion
2 cloves garlic
½ teaspoon ground coriander
1–3 chillies, seeded
2 teaspoons grated lemon peel *or* chopped lemon grass
2 tablespoons (30 ml) lemon juice *or* tamarind water
1 tablespoon roasted peanuts, coarsely ground

Garnish
2 tablespoons chopped coriander leaves

Put the selected vegetables, coconut milk and ½ teaspoon salt in a
saucepan and bring to a low boil. Reduce the heat and simmer
until the vegetables are just tender. During this time dissolve the
creamed coconut in the water in a small pan and bring to a slow
simmer. Put the onion, garlic, coriander, chillies and lemon peel
in a food blender and grind to a smooth paste. To ensure
smoothness, add a little of the coconut milk from the vegetable
pan if necessary. Transfer the paste to the simmering coconut
cream and stir it in. Stir and simmer until the mixture starts to
thicken as the water evaporates and oil from the coconut cream is
released. Stir this paste, the lemon juice and ground peanuts into
the vegetables in the pan and transfer to a serving dish. Garnish
with coriander leaves and serve.

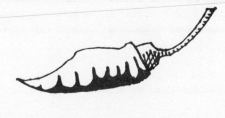

Beef and Chilli Salad   *Serves 4*

Beef salad is popular served with beer in Thailand. Thin slices of
roast beef are dressed with a hot, chilli/garlic sauce and garnished.

8 oz (225 g) roast beef sliced into thin strips 2 in (5 cm) by ½ in
  (1.25 cm)
3 cloves garlic, crushed
6 black peppercorns, freshly ground
2 teaspoons (10 ml) fish sauce *or* soya sauce
1 tablespoon (15 ml) lemon *or* lime juice
2 teaspoons sugar
2 spring onions, finely chopped
3–6 red *or* green (according to taste) fresh chillies, seeded and
  finely sliced

Garnish
lettuce leaves
coriander leaves
½ cucumber, sliced
4 tomatoes, quartered

Put the beef in a mixing bowl. Grind the garlic and black pepper
into a paste in a pestle and mortar. Add to the paste the fish sauce,
lemon juice and sugar and stir them in the mortar until well
mixed. Pour this dressing over the beef. Stir in the spring onions
and chillies. Arrange a bed of lettuce leaves on a serving dish.
Sprinkle coriander leaves over them and then arrange the beef and
dressing on top. Arrange cucumber slices and tomato quarters
around the beef and serve.

Pork and Green Apple Salad   *Serves 4*

Green mangoes would be used in this salad in Thailand, but if
they are unavailable tart green apples such as Granny Smiths
make a fine substitute. Fruit is often included in salads in Thai
cuisine.

2 tart Granny Smith apples, peeled, cored and thinly sliced
½ teaspoon salt
juice of 1 lemon
1 tablespoon (15 ml) peanut oil *or* other vegetable oil
2 cloves garlic, crushed
4 oz (100 g) minced lean pork
4 oz (100 g) cooked prawns *or* shrimps

1 teaspoon sugar
1 tablespoon (15 ml) fish sauce
1 tablespoon roasted peanuts, coarsely ground

Put the apple slices in a mixing bowl and sprinkle with salt and the juice of ½ lemon. Set aside. Heat the oil in a small frying pan and fry the garlic golden. Add the minced pork and stir-fry until brown and cooked. Remove from the heat. Combine the remaining lemon juice, the prawns, sugar, fish sauce and peanuts and pour the mixture over the apple slices. Stir in the pork, toss well and serve.

Variation
Add to the salad 1 small pineapple, peeled, sliced and then diced.

Pork and Cabbage Salad   *Serves 4*

Replace the apple in the salad above with 1 small white cabbage, blanched and finely chopped.

Grapefruit and Coconut Salad   *Serves 4*

Serve as a starter or side dish. If they are available pomelos may be
substituted for the grapefruit.

4 oz (100 g) desiccated coconut
1 teaspoon sugar
2 teaspoons (10 ml) fish sauce *or* soya sauce
2 tablespoons (30 ml) lemon juice *or* tamarind water
2 tablespoons (30 ml) water
2 teaspoons (10 ml) vegetable oil
1 clove garlic, crushed
2 tablespoons finely diced onion
2 large grapefruit, peeled and segmented

Garnish

lettuce leaves

Dry roast the coconut in a frying pan until it just starts to brown.
Turn it into a mixing bowl and stir in the sugar, fish sauce, lemon
juice and water. Heat the oil in a small pan and stir-fry the garlic
and onion until golden. Stir this mixture into the coconut.
Arrange the grapefruit segments on a few lettuce leaves on
individual plates. Pour some of the coconut dressing over each
and serve.

Prawn, Watercress and Peanut Salad   *Serves 4*

2 tablespoons (30 ml) vegetable oil
2 tablespoons finely diced onion
2 cloves garlic, crushed
1 tablespoon (15 ml) fish sauce *or* soya sauce
2 tablespoons (30 ml) lemon *or* lime juice
1 teaspoon sugar
1 lb (450 g) shelled, cooked prawns
2 tablespoons roasted peanuts, chopped
1 bunch watercress, chopped

Garnish

2 red chillies, seeded and finely sliced (optional)

Fry the onion and garlic in the oil until golden and set aside.
Combine the fish sauce, lemon juice and sugar. Combine the
prawns, peanuts and watercress and stir into them the lemon
dressing. Transfer to a serving dish, sprinkle the garlic and onion
mixture over and garnish with chillies if used.

Fiery Fish Salad

Serves 6–8

This fish salad uses lots of chillies. If you are not used to hot food reduce the amount by a quarter or a half or even more. Serve with chilled cucumber slices for cooling the mouth.

4 fish fillets, about 8 oz (225 g) each
2 tablespoons (30 ml) vegetable oil
1 small onion *or* 3 shallots, finely sliced
1 tablespoon grated ginger root
3 oz (75 g) roasted peanuts, coarsely ground
3 tablespoons (45 ml) lemon *or* lime juice
1 teaspoon grated lemon *or* lime rind
3 red chillies, seeded and finely diced
3 green chillies, seeded and finely diced } *or* 6 red *or* green chillies
½ teaspoon salt

Garnish

lettuce leaves
finely chopped coriander leaves

Fry the fish in the oil until lightly browned on both sides and cooked. Set aside to cool. Combine all the remaining ingredients except the garnishes and mix well. Flake the fish into a mixing bowl and stir the chilli dressing into it.
Make a bed of lettuce on a serving dish, pile on the fish salad, garnish with coriander leaves and serve.

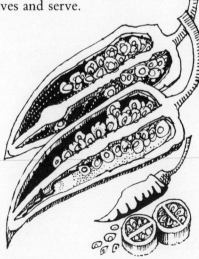

Cucumber Boats with Beef Cargo   *Serves 4–8*

Hollowed-out cucumber halves are stuffed with a mint and garlic flavoured roast-beef filling and presented on a green sea of lettuce leaves.

2 small cucumbers
1 clove garlic, finely chopped
4 tablespoons finely chopped mint leaves *or* 2 teaspoons crushed
    dried mint
2 tablespoons (30 ml) lemon *or* lime juice
1 tablespoon (15 ml) fish sauce *or* soya sauce
1 teaspoon sugar
8 oz (225 g) roast beef, thinly sliced and then shredded
salt and black pepper to taste

Garnish

lettuce leaves
sprigs of parsley *or* coriander
2–3 red chillies, seeded and finely sliced (optional)

Halve the cucumbers crosswise, then lengthwise, and scoop out the seeds to form 8 boats. Combine the garlic, mint leaves, lemon juice, fish sauce, sugar and roast beef and mix well together. Add salt (if needed at all) and black pepper to taste. Fill the cucumber boats with this mixture. Arrange them on a sea of lettuce leaves and garnish them with sprigs of parsley or coriander and a sprinkling of chillies (if used).

Big Salad   *Serves 4–8*

This is a large mixed meat and fish salad suitable to serve as a main course.

8 oz (225 g) lean cooked pork *or* beef, sliced into thin strips
8 oz (225 g) cooked chicken, sliced into thin strips
8 oz (225 g) cooked prawns *or* shrimps
1 large or 2 small cucumbers, sliced
2 oz (50 g) bean sprouts, washed and drained
4 medium tomatoes, sliced
2 tablespoons coarsely chopped mint *or* coriander leaves
salt and freshly ground black pepper to taste

Dressing

juice of 1 lemon
1 tablespoon (15 ml) fish sauce *or* soya sauce

1 teaspoon sugar
1 clove garlic, finely chopped
½–1 red chilli, seeded and finely sliced (optional)

Garnish

2 hard-boiled eggs, peeled and sliced
coriander leaves *or* mint sprigs
2 red chillies, seeded and finely sliced (optional)

Combine the pork or beef, chicken, prawns, cucumbers, bean sprouts, tomatoes, mint or coriander leaves and salt and pepper to taste in a large mixing bowl. Combine the dressing ingredients, mix well and pour them over the salad. Toss, and serve garnished with hard-boiled egg slices, coriander leaves or mint sprigs, and rings of chilli pepper if desired.

Vegetable Salad with Hot Sauce *Serves 4 or more*

For this salad, suitably cut fresh vegetables are dipped into a hot sauce and then eaten in the manner of a French *crudité*. Select a variety of vegetables from those suggested in the recipe, remembering to combine a range of textures, colours and flavours. Present them on a large serving dish around a bowl of the hot sauce.

celery, cut into sticks
cucumber, sliced
watercress, in sprigs
red radishes, whole
Chinese cabbage, coarsely
  chopped into strips
carrots, cut into sticks
green peppers, seeded and cut
  into strips

young green beans, left whole
chicory leaves
green apples, sliced and
  sprinkled with lemon juice
aubergine *or* courgette slices,
  browned in a little oil

Sauce

1 tablespoon (15 ml) fish sauce
  or soya sauce
2 oz (50 g) cooked shrimps *or*
  prawns

2 cloves garlic
juice of 1 lemon
2 teaspoons sugar
Chilli Sauce to taste

Prepare all the vegetables and chill them while you prepare the sauce. Put all the sauce ingredients into a blender and blend to a smooth, thickish consistency. Scrape into a serving bowl. Serve as described above.

Market Fare

The best dining experiences usually originate with the purchase of choice ingredients. In Thailand, this usually entails visiting local markets which, throughout the year, are supplied once, perhaps twice, daily with fresh meat, fish, poultry, vegetables, fruits, spices and flowers.

Despite refrigeration, many women make the daily pilgrimage. Anong visits at least four times weekly, claiming that refrigeration is a mixed blessing, that taste deteriorates with extended (anything over twenty-four hours) life. Certainly, she never buys from supermarkets anything she can buy fresh elsewhere.

While her stated reasons are valid, I'm certain she really enjoys the excursion, the pleasure of hard bargaining (supermarkets have fixed prices and are impersonal) and the sheer warmth of human contact and gossip.

Market shopping is a battle of wits. Unscrupulous vendors inject, say, chicken, with water to increase recorded weights, and prices fluctuate daily. Vendors endeavour to maintain high prices while shoppers naturally attempt to bargain them down. Displayed prices are merely fiction for government inspectors. Adept bargaining can fashion reductions of up to 50 per cent. Buying cheaply or cheaper without being cheated is deeply satisfying.

Urban markets are typically crowded under one roof or are in the open air, ribboned beneath awnings along narrow lanes dissecting shophouse blocks. During peak hours, all seethe with fiercely haggling humanity, exude raw vitality and cheerful, busy, busy character.

Sometimes Anong will return from her excursions complaining about rising prices, the diminishing quality of certain items and the dwindling choice of commodities sold. The latter comment strains credibility. The last time I accompanied her to the local market – something I hate (does *any* man really enjoy shopping, particularly with his wife?); she hates me coming, too, because my presence invariably raises prices – that last time I listed the items for sale, for a handbook project. I probably missed some items, but . . .

Asparagus, lentils, aubergines, marrows, cucumbers, tomatoes, peas, lettuces, cabbages, cauliflowers, celery, spinach, parsley, shallots, sprouts, cress, kale, onions, mint, radishes, potatoes, turnips, carrots, morning glory, yams, jackfruit, papayas, pomeloes, melons, coconuts, lemons, pomegranates, peanuts, durians, oranges, mangoes, water chestnuts, grapes, cashew nuts, raisins, sugar cane, maize, dried fruits, preserves, bananas, pineapples, honeycombs and wild honey, sunflower seeds, salt, fish sauce, dried prawns, shrimp paste, pepper, chillies, garlic, nutmeg, cinnamon, rice and wheat noodles, chicken, duck, pheasant, quail and turtle eggs, spiced sausages, pigs' intestines, ricebirds, field crabs, dried beetles, plucked chicken, geese, ducks, wriggling eels, venison, trussed turtles, pork, beef, mutton, dried freshwater and seawater fish, fresh catfish, perch, bass, mackerel, dogfish, plaice, carp, tuna, crayfish, prawns, crabs, squid, mussels, scallops, oysters, snails, rabbit, wild hare and boar, birds' nests, cakes, scones, bread.

Would that everyone, everywhere, enjoyed the same 'dwindling choice'. . . .

Beef & Pork Dishes

Beef with green peppers•Beef with chillies and Chinese mushrooms•Sweet and sour beef and vegetables•Hot spiced beef with mint leaves•Thai hamburgers•Rama bathing (beef in coconut milk)•Chilli beef•Thai meat balls•Sweet and sour pork and shrimps (or prawns)•Sweet pork•Deep-fried pork meat balls•Fried pork and vegetables•Fried crisp pork• Minced pork and pineapple

Thailand is traditionally more of a fish-eating nation than a meat-eating one, and meat dishes are still considered something of a treat. The pork or beef (more usually buffalo in Thailand) is usually cut and cooked in small, bite-size pieces or very thin slices, and a little goes a long way. No specific cut of meat is used, and the choice is between different qualities of lean or fatty meat. The recipes given here are all simple, quick to prepare and well flavoured. The cooking method is usually stir-frying.

Beef with Green Peppers   *Serves 4*

Serve with boiled rice.

4 tablespoons (60 ml) vegetable oil
1 tablespoon (15 ml) cooking sherry
1 teaspoon cornflour
½ teaspoon salt
1 lb (450 g) lean beef sliced very thinly and cut into ½ in (1.25 cm) by 2 in (5 cm) pieces
4 medium green peppers, seeded and thinly sliced
3–4 spring onions, thinly sliced
1 red chilli, seeded and finely sliced (optional)
1 tablespoon (15 ml) soya sauce
pinch of sugar

Garnish
finely chopped coriander leaves

Combine 1 tablespoon (15 ml) of the vegetable oil with the sherry, cornflour and salt in a bowl and mix well. Add the beef slices and stir them around to coat each piece with the marinade mixture. Set the bowl aside in the refrigerator for an hour. Heat half the remaining oil in a wok or frying pan and stir-fry the beef (drain off any marinade not absorbed, and reserve) very briefly (30 seconds). Transfer the beef back to the bowl. Heat the remaining oil in the wok or pan and stir-fry the peppers, spring onions and chilli (if used) until the peppers are just softened but still crunchy (2–3 minutes). Stir in the beef, any reserved marinade, soya sauce and sugar. Heat through, and add salt to taste if necessary. Serve garnished with coriander leaves.

Beef with Chillies and Chinese Mushrooms   *Serves 4*

Serve with boiled rice and stir-fried greens.

3 tablespoons (45 ml) vegetable oil
1 medium onion, chopped
2 cloves garlic, finely chopped
2–4 fresh *or* dried red chillies, seeded and finely chopped
1 lb (450 g) lean beef, sliced very thinly and cut into ½ in
  (1.25 cm) by 2 in (5 cm) pieces
3 fl oz (75 ml) meat stock *or* chicken stock
6 Chinese dried mushrooms, soaked for 30 minutes in hot water,
  stems discarded and caps sliced
2 tablespoons (30 ml) fish sauce *or* soya sauce
1 tablespoon (15 ml) oyster sauce (optional)
freshly ground black pepper to taste

Heat the oil in a frying pan or wok and stir-fry the onion and garlic until softened. Add the beef and chillies, and lightly brown the beef on both sides. Add the remaining ingredients, stir well and bring to a slow boil. Reduce the heat and simmer for 5 minutes or until the beef is tender. Serve immediately.

Sweet and Sour Beef and Vegetables　　　*Serves 4–6*

This recipe may also be used with lean pork or chicken.

4 tablespoons (60 ml) vegetable oil
1 lb (450 g) beef, sliced very thinly and cut into ½ in (1.25 cm)
　by 2 in (5 cm) pieces
4 cloves garlic, finely chopped
1 medium onion, chopped
2 medium green peppers, seeded and chopped
1 small to medium cucumber, sliced lengthwise in half, seeded
　and sliced
2 medium tomatoes, quartered
1–2 red chillies, seeded and finely chopped
2 tablespoons sugar
2 tablespoons (30 ml) white vinegar
2 tablespoons (30 ml) soya sauce
2 teaspoons cornflour, dissolved in 2 tablespoons (30 ml) water
2 spring onions, finely chopped

Garnish
2 tablespoons finely chopped coriander leaves

Heat the oil in a wok or large frying pan. Add the beef and lightly
brown on both sides. Lift the beef out with a slotted spoon and set
aside. Add the garlic, onion, green peppers, cucumber,
tomatoes and chillies, stir-frying for 30 seconds after the addition
of each one. Stir the beef back into the wok or pan. Combine the
sugar, vinegar, soya sauce and cornflour in a small bowl and mix
well together. Stir this mixture and the spring onions into the
beef and vegetables. Cook, stirring, until the sauce thickens.
Serve garnished with coriander leaves.

Hot Spiced Beef with Mint Leaves　　　*Serves 6*

This dish, more a salad than a cooked meal, is served as an
appetizer with drinks or as part of a larger main meal. It is very
spicy and the beef is cooked only lightly. Traditionally, buffalo
meat is used.

3 cloves garlic
2 red chillies, seeded
1 lb (450 g) minced beef
1 medium onion, finely diced
1 green pepper, seeded and finely chopped

1 tablespoon (15 ml) fish sauce
1 teaspoon freshly ground coriander seeds
1 teaspoon salt
2 tablespoons (30 ml) lemon *or* lime juice
about 20 mint leaves, half of them chopped

Garnish
cucumber slices
lemon wedges

Wrap the garlic and chillies in a piece of aluminium foil and dry roast them over a high heat until they are browned and almost burnt. Leave to cool, and then pound them together in a pestle and mortar and set aside. Put the beef without oil into a heated wok or frying pan and stir-fry over a moderate heat until the pink of the beef has just gone. Place the beef in a mixing bowl and stir in the powdered chilli and garlic, the onion, green pepper, fish sauce, coriander, salt, lemon juice and chopped mint leaves. Transfer to a serving dish, garnish with the remaining mint leaves and decorate with the cucumber slices and lemon wedges.

Thai Hamburgers   *Serves 4–6*

Serve as a change from regular hamburgers or as a main course with Cucumber Sauce (see Sauces).

12 oz (350 g) minced beef
12 oz (350 g) minced pork
4 cloves garlic, finely chopped
2 teaspoons ground coriander
1 teaspoon ground black pepper
½ teaspoon ground nutmeg
1 small onion, finely chopped
2 eggs, beaten
1 tablespoon (15 ml) fish sauce *or* soya sauce
1 tablespoon finely chopped coriander leaves *or* parsley
Oil for shallow-frying

Combine all the ingredients except the oil, and mix thoroughly by hand or in an electric mixer. Clean your hands, leave them wet and mould the mixture into hamburger-size patties. Shallow-fry them on both sides until nicely browned.

Rama bathing (Beef in Coconut Milk)   *Serves 6*

Lean, good-quality beef is cooked in coconut milk, served on a
bed of blanched spinach leaves and covered in a sauce. The origin
of the name of this dish is obscure. There was a Thai king called
Rama, and in the dish it is the beef that bathes in the coconut
sauce. Perhaps, rather like Cleopatra in her asses' milk, Rama
enjoyed a coconut-milk bath.

1½ pints (900 ml) medium coconut milk *or* 5 oz (125 g) creamed
   coconut dissolved in 1¼ pints (750 ml) hot water
1½ lb (700 g) beef cut into very thin strips
2 tablespoons (30 ml) fish sauce *or* soya sauce
1 tablespoon brown sugar
½ medium onion, chopped
2 cloves garlic
1 teaspoon finely chopped fresh ginger
1–3 red chillies, seeded
1 teaspoon cornflour, dissolved in 1 tablespoon (15 ml) water
3 tablespoons peanut butter
1 lb (450 g) fresh *or* frozen spinach, coarsely chopped
5 fl oz (125 ml) coconut cream *or* plain yoghurt

Reserve 5 fl oz (125 ml) of the coconut milk and put the remainder
in a large saucepan. Bring to the boil over a moderate heat. Add
the beef, fish sauce and sugar and gently boil for 5 minutes. Blend
the reserved coconut milk, onion, garlic, ginger, chillies,
cornflour and peanut butter into a smooth paste and stir it into the
pan. Gently simmer for 5 minutes. Blanch the spinach in boiling
water until wilted. Drain and arrange on a serving dish. With a
slotted spoon lift out the beef and arrange it over the top of the
spinach. Pour the sauce over it. Top with coconut cream or
yoghurt and serve.

Chilli Beef   *Serves 4*

Thin slices of beef marinated in a sweet ginger/garlic sauce,
stir-fried with vegetables and chillies and served over rice with a
sauce made from the marinade. Serve with boiled rice.

1 lb (450 g) lean beef, very thinly sliced and cut into ½ in
  (1.25 cm) by 2 in (5 cm) lengths
2 cloves garlic, crushed
2 teaspoons grated ginger root
1 tablespoon brown sugar
2 tablespoons (30 ml) soya sauce
4 tablespoons (60 ml) vegetable oil
1 medium onion, chopped
2 green peppers, seeded and chopped
4 oz (100 g) mushrooms, sliced
2–4 red chillies, seeded and finely chopped
6 fl oz (175 ml) meat stock
2 teaspoons cornflour dissolved in 2 tablespoons (30 ml) water
1 tablespoon (15 ml) fish sauce
2 tablespoons (30 ml) oyster sauce (optional)

Put the beef slices into a bowl. Add the garlic, ginger, sugar and
soya sauce. Mix well and set aside to marinate for 1 hour. Drain
off the beef and reserve the juices. Heat the oil in a wok or frying
pan and brown the beef on both sides, stirring all the time. Add
the onion, peppers, mushrooms and chillies and stir-fry for 2
minutes. Add the marinade juices, the stock and cornflour, mix
well and simmer for 3–4 minutes. Stir into the mixture the fish
sauce and oyster sauce. Serve immediately.

Thai Meat Balls   *Serves 6*

Serve with rice and Sweet and Sour Sauce or Peanut Butter Sauce
(see Sauces).

ingredients as for Thai hamburgers
flour for coating
oil for deep frying

Prepare the hamburger mixture as above and form it into
normal-sized meat balls. Dust the meat balls with flour and
deep-fry them golden brown.

Sweet and Sour Pork and Shrimps (or Prawns) *Serves 4*

2 tablespoons (30 ml) vegetable oil
4 cloves garlic, finely chopped
8 oz (225 g) lean pork, thinly sliced and cut into ½ in (1.25 cm)
　　by 2 in (5 cm) pieces
2 tablespoons (30 ml) fish sauce
4 tablespoons (60 ml) water *or* stock
1 tablespoon sugar
1 tablespoon (15 ml) white vinegar
8 oz (225 g) cooked shrimps *or* prawns
2 medium green peppers, seeded and thinly sliced *or* 8 oz (225 g)
　　fresh green beans, cut into 2 in (5 cm) pieces
freshly ground black pepper to taste

Heat the oil in a wok or frying pan and stir-fry the garlic until golden. Add the pork and stir-fry until browned all over. Stir in the fish sauce, water, sugar and vinegar and cook over a moderate heat for 3 minutes. Add the shrimps and green peppers, turn up the heat and stir-fry for another 3 minutes. Add black pepper to taste and serve.

Variation
Other vegetables such as cauliflower, broccoli, Chinese greens, spinach etc. may be used in this recipe.

Sweet Pork

Sweet pork is made either from pork cut into small pieces or from a single joint of pork. In the first method the sweet pork is served as a side dish, or for a light lunch with rice, and in the second in much the same way as we use cooked ham. In both cases the dish can be made ahead of time and served from the refrigerator.

Method 1   *Serves 2–3*

2 tablespoons (30 ml) vegetable oil
8 oz (225 g) lean pork, cut into bite-size pieces
1 medium onion, finely chopped
1–2 tablespoons brown sugar
2 tablespoons (30 ml) fish sauce

Garnish
finely chopped coriander leaves *or* parsley

Heat the oil in a small frying pan or wok and add the pork and onion. Stir-fry over a moderate heat until the pork is cooked. Add the sugar to taste, and the fish sauce. Stir-fry until the pork is well coated with the thick sauce that forms. Serve hot or chilled, garnished with coriander or parsley.

Method 2   *Serves 4–6*

2 lb (900 g) loin of pork   6 fl oz (175 ml) fish sauce
1 clove garlic, crushed   1¼ pints (750 ml) water
4 oz (100 g) dark brown sugar

Garnish
2 spring onions, finely chopped *or* 1 tablespoon chopped chives
finely chopped parsley

Put all the ingredients except the garnish into a large saucepan. Bring to the boil, reduce the heat, cover and simmer for 45 minutes. Uncover, skim off any fat and continue to cook over a moderate heat, uncovered, for another 15 minutes or until the pork is tender. The cooking liquid should be quite syrupy by now. Lift the pork out onto a serving dish. Serve it cut into serving pieces or whole, in each case with sauce from the pan poured over. Serve hot or chilled, garnished with chopped spring onions and parsley.

Deep-Fried Pork Meat Balls   *Serves 4*

Serve with a Sweet and Sour Sauce (see Sauces), stir-fried vegetables and rice.

1 lb (450 g) lean pork, finely minced
1 tablespoon (15 ml) lemon *or* lime juice
1 egg, beaten
½ teaspoon ground coriander
½ teaspoon salt
½ teaspoon black pepper
1 tablespoon plain flour
½ medium onion, finely chopped
2 oz (50 g) mushrooms, finely chopped
½ medium green pepper, seeded and finely chopped
oil for deep-frying

Combine the minced pork, lemon juice, egg, coriander, salt and pepper and mix them together thoroughly. Add the flour, onion, mushrooms and green pepper, mix well and form the mixture (easier with wet, clean hands) into balls about 1 in (2.5 cm) in diameter. Heat the oil until it barely starts to smoke, and deep-fry the meat balls until nicely browned. Serve immediately.

Fried Pork and Vegetables   *Serves 4*

4 oz (100 g) mushrooms, sliced
4 oz (100 g) cabbage, finely shredded
4 oz (100 g) fresh green beans, cut into 2 in (5 cm) lengths
2 tablespoons (30 ml) vegetable oil
6 cloves garlic, finely chopped
8 oz (225 g) lean pork, sliced very thinly and cut into ½ in (1.25 cm) by 2 in (5 cm) pieces
3 tablespoons (45 ml) fish sauce
1 teaspoon sugar

Garnish
finely chopped fresh mint *or* crushed dried mint

Cover the mushrooms, cabbage and green beans in cold water and set aside. Heat the oil in a frying pan or wok and stir-fry the garlic until golden. Add the pork and brown it all over. Drain off the mushrooms and vegetables and stir them into the pan or wok. Fry for 3 minutes. Sprinkle with fish sauce and sugar, toss everything together and serve garnished with mint.

Fried Crisp Pork — *Serves 4*

Slices of belly pork are deep-fried, diced and then refried with spices and vegetables in a hot sauce. Serve with boiled rice.

oil for deep-frying
12 oz (350 g) belly pork with skin, cut into ¾ in (2 cm) strips
1 medium onion, finely chopped
2 cloves garlic, finely chopped
2 teaspoons grated fresh ginger root
1–2 red or green chillies, seeded and finely chopped
2 medium tomatoes, quartered
1 teaspoon finely chopped coriander root (optional)
2 tablespoons (30 ml) soya sauce
1 tablespoon (15 ml) cooking sherry
3 tablespoons (45 ml) stock *or* water
black pepper to taste
1 tablespoon (15 ml) fish sauce

Garnish
finely chopped coriander leaves

Heat the oil until it barely begins to smoke and then deep-fry the belly pork until nicely browned and crisp. Remove from the oil, drain and allow to cool. Now chop the pork into small, bite-size pieces and set aside. Heat 2 tablespoons (30 ml) vegetable oil in a wok or frying pan and stir-fry the onion, garlic and ginger until the onion is softened and lightly browned. Add the chillies, tomatoes, coriander root, soya sauce, cooking sherry and stock. Mix well and add black pepper to taste. Add the pork and bring the mixture to the boil. Reduce the heat and simmer over a low heat, covered, for 10 minutes. Add the fish sauce, stir and simmer a further 5 minutes. Serve garnished with coriander leaves.

Minced Pork and Pineapple   *Serves 4*

This dish may be served hot with rice or cold as a salad.

2 tablespoons (30 ml) vegetable oil
2 cloves garlic, crushed
1 lb (450 g) lean minced pork
½ red chilli, seeded and finely chopped
2 oz (50 g) roasted peanuts, coarsely crushed *or* 2 tablespoons
    crunchy peanut butter
1 tablespoon (15 ml) fish sauce *or* soya sauce
1 teaspoon ground coriander seeds
1 medium fresh pineapple, peeled, cored and cut into chunks *or*
    10 oz (300 g) tinned pineapple chunks

Garnish
finely chopped coriander leaves

Heat the oil in a frying pan or wok and stir-fry the garlic until
golden. Add the pork and chilli, if used, and stir-fry for 5
minutes. Stir in the peanuts, fish sauce and coriander. Simmer,
with frequent stirring, for 10 minutes. If the dish is to be served
hot, add the pineapple, heat through and serve. Otherwise, turn
the pork mixture into a bowl and set aside to cool to room
temperature. Stir in the cold pineapple chunks and serve. In each
case garnish with coriander leaves.

Putrid Pisces

Thailand's north-east, a sprawling plateau largely bordered by the Mekong River and Laos, is home of some of Thailand's tastiest and more unusual food. Perennial favourites include fiery minced specialities, lavishly spiced salads, and truly incomparable grilled chicken. I'm familiar with these, and many more, partly because I travel regularly to the north-east, mostly because Anong hails from the area.

One of the most popular north-east dishes, enjoyed throughout Thailand, is the famous (or infamous) *Pla Ra* (Fermented Fish). Anong and her family relish it so much that it forms part of their daily diet.

Fermented fish is rarely enjoyed by Europeans. A major obstacle is that it presents itself as a totally offensive concoction. The smell alone recalls the accumulated stench of putrefying corpses, abandoned kennels, dirty feet, stagnant bilges and fly-blown offal. (In fairness, many Thais, Anong included, find the smell of Danish blue cheese equally outrageous.)

The dish is easily made. Freshwater fish – from ponds, canals, streams, flooded fields or ditches – are cleaned, beheaded, descaled, gutted, salted and placed in sealed earthenware jars. After a few days, a fine powder made from fried rice grains is added. Flesh rots, natural juices ferment in darkness. The parthenogenesis is ready to eat after one week, or when it is appropriately salty and sour. Anong informs me that connoisseurs wait for one month, even one year, after which everything is particularly rotten. It can then be eaten boiled or raw.

Fermented fish enhances or is the major ingredient of piquant soups, salads and immensely popular chilli pastes. Alternatively, it can be eaten just as it slimily, pungently, sibilantly, drippingly is.

And the taste?

D-e-l-i-c-i-o-u-s!

Fish & Seafood Dishes

Fried fish with various sauces•Chilli sauce•Sweet and sour
fish sauce•Ginger sauce•Thai fish cakes•Shrimp or prawn
toast•Fried fillet in lemon sauce•Fish fillets with Chinese
mushrooms•Crisp fried fish with curry sauce•Prawns with
stir-fried vegetables and pineapple•Simmered fish in red
sauce•Prawn and aubergine curry•Deep-fried stuffed crabs•
Grilled mackerel with hot sauce•Simple fried fish

Thailand, criss-crossed with inland waterways and canals, with
access to the Indian Ocean and the Gulf of Thailand and covered
in a patchwork quilt of seasonally flooded paddy fields, is blessed
with an abundance of seafood and fish. In the country areas the
peasants can catch their fish fresh as needed, and in the towns the
daily markets and numerous seafood restaurants provide fresh
fish and fish dishes in myriad variety seven days a week.

The dishes I have chosen for this chapter are designed to be
used with commonly available fish and fish fillets. The cooking
method is mainly frying, and the fish are served in a variety of
tasty sauces. Other seafood recipes are given in the chapters on
Starters or Side Dishes, and Curry Dishes.

Fried Fish with Various Sauces *Serves 4*

The fish is fried and then served with a choice of sauces. The method is suitable for one large fish or for 3 or 4 lighter, smaller fish. Three sauce recipes are given – Chilli, Sweet and Sour and Ginger. Choose whichever you prefer. For those on a reduced fat diet, the fish could be steamed first and then served with one of the sauces.

2 lb (900 g) whole round fish (a single fish such as mullet or 2–4 smaller ones such as trout), cleaned and gutted
3 tablespoons plain flour, seasoned to taste with salt and black pepper
4 fl oz (100 ml) vegetable oil
choice of sauce (see below)

Choice of garnishes
finely chopped spring onion
red or green chillies, seeded and finely chopped
finely chopped coriander leaves
2 oz (50 g) dried onion flakes browned in 1 tablespoon (15 ml) vegetable oil

Pre-heat the oven to 350° F (180° C, gas mark 4). Score the skin of the fish 2 or 3 times on each side and dust with the seasoned flour. Heat the oil in a wok or large frying pan and fry the fish, individually, golden brown and crisp on both sides. Drain the fish of excess oil and set them aside to keep hot in the pre-heated oven. Prepare the sauce of your choice.

Chilli Sauce

2 tablespoons (30 ml) vegetable oil that the fish was fried in
1 tablespoon finely chopped coriander leaves
½ medium onion, finely chopped
1 teaspoon ground coriander
2–5 red chillies (according to taste), seeded and finely chopped
2 tablespoons sugar
2 tablespoons (30 ml) fish sauce
2 teaspoons cornflour creamed with 4 fl oz (100 ml) water

Pour out of the wok or frying pan the oil in which the fish was fried, leaving about 2 tablespoons (30 ml) behind. Stir-fry the coriander leaves, onion, ground coriander and chillies until the onion is lightly browned. Add the sugar, the fish sauce, and the cornflour and water mix. Stir well and simmer for 2 minutes or until the sauce thickens. Pour the sauce over the fish and serve garnished.

Sweet and Sour Fish Sauce

2 teaspoons cornflour
3 tablespoons (45 ml) water
1 tablespoon tomato purée
1 tablespoon (15 ml) rice vinegar *or* other vinegar
2 teaspoons (10 ml) soya sauce
2 tablespoons sugar
salt to taste
2 tablespoons (30 ml) vegetable oil that the fish was fried in
1 medium onion, finely chopped
2 medium tomatoes, chopped small
2 oz (50 g) mushrooms, chopped small

Combine the cornflour, water, tomato purée, vinegar, soya sauce and sugar, add salt to taste and mix into a smooth sauce. Heat the oil in a wok or frying pan and stir-fry the onion until golden. Add the tomatoes and mushrooms, stir-fry a further 2 minutes and then add the prepared sauce mixture. Stir until it thickens. Pour the sauce over the fried fish and serve garnished.

Ginger Sauce

1 tablespoon (15 ml) vegetable oil that the fish was fried in
2 tablespoons finely chopped onion
1 tablespoon finely grated ginger root
3 cloves garlic, crushed
1 tablespoon (15 ml) white vinegar
1 tablespoon brown sugar
2 tablespoons (30 ml) soya sauce
2 tablespoons (30 ml) fish sauce

Heat the oil in a wok or small frying pan, add the onion, ginger and garlic, and stir-fry until the onion is golden. Add the remaining ingredients and cook and stir for another minute or two. Pour the sauce over the fish and serve garnished.

Thai Fish Cakes   *Serves 2–3*

Serve the fish cakes with Cucumber salad sauce as a side dish and, if you wish, Hot fish sauce poured over (see Sauces).

8 oz (225 g) fish fillets
3 tablespoons (45 ml) medium coconut milk *or* plain yoghurt
½–1 teaspoon (2.5–5 ml) hot pepper sauce
1 tablespoon (15 ml) soya sauce
1 egg beaten with 1 tablespoon cornflour
2 oz (50 g) fresh green beans, chopped very small, *or* green or
  red peppers
black pepper to taste
oil for shallow-frying

Garnish

tomato wedges
lemon wedges

Lightly grill the fish fillets on both sides (about 1 minute each side under a medium grill). Flake the fish into small pieces in a mixing bowl and stir in the coconut milk or yoghurt, hot pepper sauce, soya sauce, egg and cornflour and green beans. Add black pepper to taste and thoroughly combine the mixture. Form into small, flattish fish cakes and shallow-fry golden brown on both sides. Serve garnished with tomato and lemon wedges, accompanied by the sauces mentioned above.

Shrimp or Prawn Toast   *Serves 4 as a starter*

Shrimp paste is spread on slices of bread which are then deep-fried. Shrimp toast is good as a starter or snack, or as part of a main meal or buffet.

8 oz (225 g) cooked shrimps *or* prawns
1 egg white
1 tablespoon (15 ml) fish sauce
2 teaspoons cornflour
2 teaspoons chopped onion
½ teaspoon grated ginger root
6 thin slices of bread, crusts removed
oil for deep-frying

Garnish

sprigs of coriander

Put all the ingredients except the bread and oil into a blender, and blend to form a smooth paste. Cut the bread slices into four squares and spread each one with some of the shrimp or prawn paste. Heat the oil in a wok or deep frying pan over a medium heat. Carefully lower in a batch of the bread squares and deep-fry them for 7–8 minutes, turning once, or until the bread is golden brown. Remove them with a slotted spoon, reheat the oil and do another batch. Garnish the toasts with sprigs of coriander and serve.

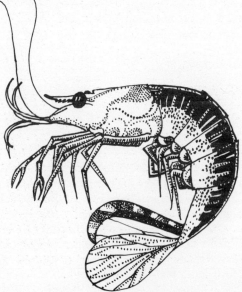

Fried Fillet in Lemon Sauce　　　　*Serves 4*

4 fl oz (100 ml) vegetable oil
1–1½ lb (450–700 g) fish fillets
2 cloves garlic, crushed
1 tablespoon brown sugar
3 tablespoons (45 ml) lemon *or* lime juice
2 teaspoons finely grated ginger root
2 spring onions, finely chopped
1 tablespoon (15 ml) soya sauce
2 tablespoons (30 ml) fish sauce

Garnish
coriander leaves
chillies, seeded and chopped

Heat the oil over a high heat in a wok or frying pan and fry the fish
fillets for 1 minute each side. Set them aside to drain, and pour off
from the wok or pan all the frying oil except for 1 tablespoon
(15 ml). Add the garlic and fry until golden. Add the sugar,
lemon juice, ginger, spring onions, soya sauce and fish sauce. Stir
well and cook over a moderate heat for 2 minutes. Carefully put
the fish fillets back into the pan and heat them through, spooning
the sauce over them. Transfer the fish to a serving dish, pour the
sauce over them, garnish with coriander and chillies (if used) and
serve.

Fish Fillets with Chinese Mushrooms   *Serves 4*

Serve with boiled rice.

3 tablespoons (45 ml) vegetable oil
2 cloves garlic, crushed
2 teaspoons finely grated ginger root
12 oz (350 g) fish fillets, cut into thick slices
4 Chinese dried mushrooms, soaked in hot water for 30 minutes,
   drained, stems discarded, caps sliced
4 oz mange tout or snow peas (optional)
1–2 red *or* green chillies, seeded and finely chopped
2 tablespoons (30 ml) fish sauce
2 teaspoons white sugar
2 spring onions, finely chopped

Garnish
sprigs of parsley *or* coriander

Heat the oil in a wok or frying pan and add the garlic and ginger.
Stir-fry until the garlic is golden. Add the fish slices, mushrooms
and mange tout. Cook over a moderate heat, stirring occasionally, until the fish is tender but still firm. Add all the remaining
ingredients except the garnish, and gently stir them in. Cook a
further 2 minutes, and then serve garnished with parsley or
coriander sprigs.

Crisp Fried Fish with Curry Sauce   *Serves 4*

4 tablespoons (60 ml) vegetable oil
1–2 tablespoons (15–30 ml) Orange *or* Mild curry paste (see
   Curry Dishes)
12 fl oz (350 ml) medium coconut milk (see page 19)
2 tablespoons (30 ml) fish sauce
1 tablespoon sugar
1½–2 lb (700–900 g) whole round fish such as trout, *or* 2 fish
   weighing the same total amount, cleaned, scaled and scored
   several times both sides
2 oz (50 g) plain flour

Garnish
finely chopped coriander leaves

Heat 1 tablespoon (15 ml) of the oil in a wok or small pan, and
stir-fry the curry paste for 3 to 4 minutes. Set aside, and in

another small pan bring the coconut milk to the boil, stirring continuously. Stir in the fried curry paste, fish sauce and sugar. Reduce the heat to very low and set to simmer, uncovered. Roll the fish in the flour. Heat the remaining oil in a wok or large frying pan over a high flame. Fry the fish on both sides until tender, crispy and browned. Transfer to a serving dish. Pour over it the curry sauce, garnish with coriander leaves and serve.

Prawns with Stir-Fried
Vegetables and Pineapple   *Serves 4–6*

1 lb (450 g) shelled prawns
salt and black pepper
2 tablespoons (30 ml) rice vinegar *or* cider vinegar
juice of 1 lemon
3 tablespoons (45 ml) vegetable oil
1 medium onion, chopped
2 cloves garlic, crushed
1 medium green pepper, seeded and cut into strips
¼–½ cucumber, peeled, sliced in half lengthwise, seeded and
    chopped
2 medium tomatoes, blanched, peeled and chopped
2 tablespoons tomato purée
1 tablespoon (15 ml) fish sauce
1 tablespoon (15 ml) soya sauce
4 oz (100 g) fresh *or* canned pineapple chunks
4 tablespoons (60 ml) stock *or* water
2 teaspoons cornflour creamed with 1 tablespoon (15 ml) water

Garnish

chopped coriander leaves

Put the prawns in a bowl and season with salt and black pepper. Stir in the vinegar and lemon juice and set aside to marinate for 15–30 minutes. Strain off the prawns and reserve the marinade. Heat the oil in a wok or large frying pan. Add the onion and garlic and stir-fry until the onion is softened. Add the prawns and stir-fry for 2–3 minutes. Add the green pepper, cucumber and tomatoes in that order, stir-frying for 1 minute after the addition of each. Add all the remaining ingredients except the cornflour and garnish. Stir well and cook over a moderate heat for another 3 minutes. Stir into the pan the cornflour and water mix. Cook and stir until the sauce thickens. Serve garnished with coriander leaves.

Simmered Fish in Red Sauce   *Serves 4*

3 tablespoons (45 ml) vegetable oil
1 medium onion, chopped
3 cloves garlic, crushed
½–1 red chilli, seeded and finely chopped
8 oz (225 g) tomatoes, blanched, peeled and chopped
2 tablespoons (30 ml) rice vinegar *or* cider vinegar
2 tablespoons tomato ketchup *or* purée
4 tablespoons (60 ml) water
salt and freshly milled black pepper to taste
1–1½ lb (450–700 g) fish fillets, skinned *or* 1–2 whole fish,
    gutted and cleaned

Garnish
finely chopped coriander leaves

Heat the oil in a wok or frying pan. Add the onion, garlic and
chilli and stir-fry until the onion is golden. Reduce the heat and
add the tomatoes, vinegar, ketchup and water. Cook, stirring
occasionally, until the tomatoes have pulped. Season to taste with
salt and black pepper, and then gently place the fish into the
simmering sauce. Baste the fish with the sauce, cover the pan and
simmer until the fish is tender (15–20 minutes). Serve garnished
liberally with coriander leaves.

Prawn and Aubergine Curry   *Serves 4*

1 lb (450 g) shelled prawns
1–2 red chillies, seeded and finely chopped
1 teaspoon turmeric
1 teaspoon ground coriander seeds
2 teaspoons grated ginger root
2 cloves garlic, finely chopped
3 tablespoons (45 ml) vegetable oil
1 medium onion, finely chopped
1 medium aubergine, finely chopped, salted, pressed for
    30 minutes and drained
8 fl oz (225 ml) coconut milk *or* 2 oz (50 g) creamed coconut
    dissolved in 6 fl oz (175 ml) hot water
1 tablespoon (15 ml) soya sauce *or* fish sauce

Garnish
lemon wedges

Put the prawns in a bowl and add the chillies, turmeric, coriander, ginger and garlic. Mix well and set aside in the refrigerator to marinate for 1 hour. Heat the oil in a wok or large frying pan and stir-fry the onion golden. Add the aubergine pieces and stir-fry until almost tender. Add the prawn mixture, mix well and stir-fry for 1 minute. Pour in the coconut milk and soya sauce, and simmer over a low heat, uncovered, for 10 minutes, stirring occasionally. Serve over rice garnished with lemon wedges.

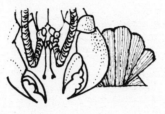

Deep-Fried Stuffed Crabs   *Serves 4*

4 small fresh crabs
1 tablespoon finely chopped onion
3 cloves garlic, finely chopped
2 tablespoons finely chopped coriander leaves
salt and black pepper to taste
4 tablespoons (60 ml) coconut milk *or* cow's milk if unavailable
1 tablespoon (15 ml) fish sauce
2 egg whites, beaten stiff
1 egg yolk
oil for deep-frying

Put the crabs in a large pot of salted boiling water and simmer for 15 minutes. Lift them out of the pot and set aside to cool. Remove the legs and claws and take off the top shells. Extract all the crab meat from the various parts and set aside. Clean the shells ready for stuffing. Combine the crab meat with the onion, garlic and half the coriander leaves, and season to taste with salt and black pepper. Stir into this mixture the coconut milk, fish sauce and beaten egg whites and mix well. Stuff the crab shells with the mixture and brush the top of the stuffing with egg yolk. Heat the oil over a medium heat and lower the crabs one or two at a time into the hot oil, shell side down, and deep-fry for 3–4 minutes or until golden brown. Serve garnished with the remaining coriander leaves.

Grilled Mackerel with Hot Sauce   *Serves 4*

This is a typical South-East Asian method of grilling fish, but the recipe is given its Thai flavour by fish sauce and coriander leaves.

4 medium mackerel, cleaned and gutted
salt to taste
juice of 1 lemon

Marinade

2 cloves garlic, crushed
2 tablespoons (30 ml) fish sauce
2 teaspoons dark brown sugar
1 teaspoon (5 ml) water

Sauce

1 tablespoon melted butter
1 tablespoon (15 ml) soya sauce
½–1 small dried *or* fresh red chilli, seeded and finely chopped
1 small onion, finely chopped and fried brown in 1 tablespoon
    (15 ml) vegetable oil

Garnish

coriander leaves

Dry the fish, score the skins 2 or 3 times with a sharp knife, season the fish with salt and sprinkle them with half the lemon juice. Combine the marinade ingredients in a shallow dish and put the fish in. Brush them with the marinade and leave them to marinate for 30 minutes or longer. Remove the fish and grill them under a hot grill for 10 minutes, turning 3–4 times and basting them with any leftover marinade. Put the fish on a serving dish and pour over it a little melted butter. Quickly whisk together the remaining sauce ingredients, pour the sauce over the fish and garnish with coriander leaves. Serve immediately.

Simple Fried Fish   *Serves 4*

Trout is used in the recipe given here, but any available round fish
of the right size may be cooked by this method.

4 medium trout, gutted and cleaned
½ teaspoon ground turmeric
1 teaspoon salt
4 fl oz (100 ml) vegetable oil
Hot Fish Sauce (*Nam Prik*) (optional; see Sauces)

Dry the skin of the fish with a paper towel. In a pestle and mortar,
or with the back of a spoon, rub the turmeric and salt together.
With your fingers rub this mixture over the skin of each fish.
Heat the oil in a wok or frying pan over a high heat and fry the fish
(in batches) for 1 minute each side. Drain, and serve with a side
dish of Hot Fish Sauce.

Travel Nosh

There are no more ardent tourists throughout Thailand than the Thais themselves. Combine the Thai love of travel with the national love of eating, and conditions are ideal for finding fine food in even the remotest corners of the country.

There's a theory that patriotism stems from a happy childhood. That may be so, but in Thailand patriotism is more likely to stem from a contented childhood stomach – particularly a contented *well-travelled* childhood stomach – than any other youthful experience(s).

As Thais instinctively know, the way to any Thai's heart is through his/her stomach; the way to his/her respect is through his/her stomach; the way to his/her mind is through his/her stomach; the development of contentment, tolerance, obedience, affection, empathy, and so on is through his/her stomach; and if he/she didn't have a stomach, he/she would be damnably difficult to coerce, let alone control.

That established, the most appreciated travel souvenirs and gifts to family and friends are those that can be eaten, gobbled, savoured and scoffed. More permanent, more expensive offerings are less favoured than, say, spicy sausages and crispened pork fat from the north and north-east, fresh oysters and cashew nuts from the south, fish sauce and dried sea products from the east, and preserves, sweetmeats and fresh fruits from the central plains.

I travel often, extensively, throughout Thailand. There was a time when I felt I shouldn't – Anong should have – because it placed dreadful strains on our marriage.

Not being a native, my biggest shortcoming was either that I forgot to buy nosh souvenirs – which caused disappointment – or that I bought inferior, expensive items that confirmed my Occidental naïvety – which caused disappointment and provoked choice fifteen-syllable obscenities – or I gave money to Thai travelling companions to purchase items for me – which caused disappointment because I'd shirked my responsibilities, and provoked choice twenty-syllable profanities in two languages, nine dialects, and myriad thunderous moods.

It took time to twig that if you are a Thai and can't travel somewhere yourself, the next best thing is to eat something from there – which affords vicarious pleasure and which is an experience shared. Nowadays I purchase souvenirs myself, always of things I have eaten at the place of purchase. Which makes Anong an unusual Oriental version of the armchair traveller. She has a *well-travelled* stomach without actually having had to undergo the discomforts of travel. Paradise. . . .

Culinary Soloists

Can you remember the comic book illustrations of one-man bands where bulbous-nosed, moustached eccentrics, aided by strategically placed pulleys, dextrously, simultaneously, played a trumpet, accordion, bass drum, cymbals, hooters and various horns?

Thai male and female food vendors who ply residential lanes – and who can provide breakfast, lunch, dinner and supper and all desirable snacks – frequently remind me of those childhood caricatures as they employ various trolleys, pushcarts, pedicarts and yokes to transport their singular kitchens/restaurants.

Allied eccentricity, blithe spirit, even musical accompaniment underline the parallels. Many vendors advertise themselves with bells, hooters, or sticks rhythmically beaten against open-ended bamboos. Others voice repetitive five- to 10-second cries and chants that have evolved into haunting vocal paradigms resembling the spontaneous scatalogical efforts of suitably stoned singers.

Aural rhythms are initially more arresting than the physical variety. Nevertheless, the latter gradually predominate, particularly the frenetic swivel-hipped gait of vendors who shoulder grotesquely weighted yokes. Bouncing panniers, buttocks, abdominal gyrations, sarong ripples, changing shoulder levels unite in syncopated harmony.

Further physical rhythms manifest once vendors have parked, preparing their specialities – their salads, their noodles, their curries, their grilled chicken and sausages, their savoury dumplings, their fresh fruit, their sweetmeats. . . . Noodle vendors, for example, fluidly sprinkle herbs and spices into empty bowls, dip noodles into steaming vats, lightly toss the resultant tangle with an economical wrist-flick into the bowl, bomb meat balls, fish balls, flood everything with boiling water, saturate with garnish, and serve in a kinetic cycle repeatedly re-enacted until their customers depart.

Women who prepare fiery salads cheerfully use lethal knives to chop lethal chillies into miniature cartwheel segments. Were their actions not spontaneous, natural, they would probably serve sliced fingertips with their specialities – which habitually numb, anaesthetize the area between cheeks and nose and chin so effectively that teeth could probably be painlessly extracted.

The vendors are valued as much for their companionship (and ability to convey, exchange, transmit and clarify gossip) as the convenience they offer. Besides, how often do appreciative diners have the opportunity of simultaneously complimenting the *maître d'* and chef, or personally asking the chef for culinary favours?

The vendors are probably doomed to go the way of the dodo, but in a sanitized age where the global village rapidly shrinks, and apelike conformity grows, it is satisfying to know that individuality, the personal touch, still survives, that solo efforts flourish.

It would be nice to believe it will ever remain so.

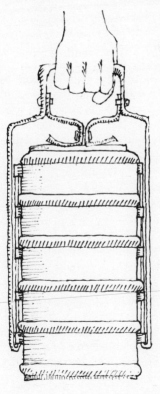

Chicken Dishes

Lemon and ginger fried chicken and mushrooms•Chicken with basil and chilli•Whole chicken simmered in spiced coconut milk• Spiced chicken with cabbage•Marinated soya fried chicken•Sweet and sour chicken•Marinated coriander fried chicken•Chicken Satay•Chicken in coconut sauce•Won-ton chicken•Chicken and spinach in peanut sauce

Chicken is eaten more often than beef or pork in the Thai diet. It is cheaper than meat, and chicken snacks are a great favourite as a street food bought barbecued from roadside vendors. Chicken Satay, for which a recipe is given here, is especially popular and a must if you ever have the luck to visit Thailand.

Most of the recipes given here are at their best and easiest if you use good-quality roasting or frying chicken, since cooking times are often short. With one exception the chicken is not cooked whole but cut into pieces. You may use a whole chicken divided into 10 pieces or more (see Cooks' Notes for the method) or a number of the same joints (legs, wings, breast, etc.) cut up. If you have a kind butcher, or the skill yourself, you may bone the pieces and use bite-size chunks of boneless chicken in the recipes. This is not essential, however, except for Chicken Satay. Without exception the recipes are delicious and usually appealing to Western tastes.

Lemon and Ginger Fried Chicken and Mushrooms
Serves 4

3 tablespoons (45 ml) vegetable oil
2 teaspoons finely chopped ginger root
4 cloves garlic, crushed
1 red chilli, seeded and finely chopped (optional)
approx. 3 lb (1.4 kg) frying chicken, cut into pieces (see Cooks' Notes) *or* 4 legs, thighs or ½ breasts of chicken each cut into 2 pieces

8 Chinese dried mushrooms, soaked in hot water for 30 minutes,
    drained, stems removed and discarded, caps sliced *or* 8 oz
    (225 g) fresh mushrooms, chopped
2 tablespoons (30 ml) lemon juice
2 teaspoons grated lemon rind
6 fl oz (175 ml) chicken stock *or* water
2 tablespoons (30 ml) fish sauce
freshly ground black pepper to taste

Garnish

finely chopped coriander leaves

Heat the oil in a wok or large saucepan and stir-fry the ginger,
garlic and chilli until the garlic is just golden. Add the chicken
pieces and fry them, with regular stirring, over medium heat
until nicely browned all over. Add the mushrooms, lemon juice,
lemon rind, stock or water, fish sauce and black pepper to taste.
Mix well, cover and cook over a moderate heat, with occasional
stirring, for 10 minutes or until the chicken is tender. Serve
garnished with coriander leaves.

Chicken with Basil and Chilli   *Serves 4*

This recipe uses sweet basil leaves; if they are unavailable fresh
mint leaves may be substituted.

3 tablespoons (45 ml) vegetable oil
4 cloves garlic, finely chopped
1–3 red chillies, seeded and finely chopped
4 chicken joints for frying (legs, wings etc.), boned if you
    wish, cut into 2 pieces
3 tablespoons sweet basil leaves
2 tablespoons (30 ml) fish sauce
1 teaspoon sugar

Heat the oil in a wok or frying pan. Add the garlic and chillies and
stir-fry the garlic until golden. Add the chicken, brown both
sides of each piece and cook, stirring occasionally and turning
over until the chicken is tender. Stir in the basil leaves, fish sauce
and sugar. Serve immediately.

Variation

Fish fillets, slices of lean meat and shelled prawns may also be
cooked in this manner.

Whole Chicken Simmered in Spiced Coconut Milk

Serves 6

This is a very tasty and simple way of preparing whole chicken. The recipe involves quite a few ingredients, but they are easy to obtain and the cooking method involves only two stages.

3–4 lb (1.4–1.8 kg) young chicken
2 tablespoons grated onion
2 red *or* green chilli peppers, seeded
3 cloves garlic
1 tablespoon peanut butter
2 teaspoons grated lemon rind
2 tablespoons (30 ml) fish sauce
1 teaspoon black pepper
1 teaspoon ground cumin
½ teaspoon ground ginger
16 fl oz (450 ml) medium coconut milk *or* 3 oz (75 g) creamed
  coconut dissolved in 12 fl oz (350 ml) hot water
4 fl oz (100 ml) coconut cream *or* single cream

Garnish
dried red chillies, seeded, finely chopped (optional)
1 teaspoon ground coriander

Put the chicken into a large saucepan. Put all the other ingredients except the last four into a blender. Blend to a smooth paste. Add a little of the coconut milk to make the paste thinner and then stir it into the coconut milk. Pour this mixture over the chicken, bring to the boil, reduce the heat, cover the pan and simmer for 45–50 minutes or until the chicken is tender. During this time turn the chicken 2 or 3 times. Transfer the chicken to a warmed serving dish. Stir the coconut cream or cream into the sauce left in the pan. Stir and cook over a low heat for 2–3 minutes. Pour the sauce over the chicken, and garnish with chopped chillies and coriander.

Spiced Chicken with Cabbage

Serves 4

Chicken and cabbage are unusual partners but together in this recipe they make a crunchy, spicy, filling dish. A curried variation is also given.

3 tablespoons (45 ml) vegetable oil
4 cloves garlic, crushed

4 joints of chicken (legs, wings etc.) weighing about 2 lb (900 g)
1 teaspoon ground coriander
1 teaspoon freshly ground black pepper
salt to taste
2 tablespoons (30 ml) fish sauce *or* soya sauce
2 teaspoons sugar
10 fl oz (300 ml) stock *or* water
6 oz (175 g) cabbage, coarsely chopped
8 fl oz (225 ml) thick coconut milk *or* sour cream

Heat the oil in a wok or large saucepan and fry the garlic until golden. Add the chicken pieces and brown them on both sides. Push the chicken pieces to one side in the wok or pan and stir in the coriander, pepper, salt, fish sauce, sugar and stock. Rearrange the chicken pieces and bring to the boil, reduce the heat, cover and simmer until the chicken is tender. Add the cabbage and mix in. Cook and stir until the cabbage is tender but still crunchy. Transfer the chicken pieces and cabbage to a warmed serving dish. Stir the coconut milk into the pan or wok. Heat the mixture through, pour it over the chicken and serve.

Variation

Stir 1 tablespoon (15 ml) of curry paste (see Curry Dishes) into 1 tablespoon (15 ml) lemon juice and 1 tablespoon (15 ml) fish sauce or soya sauce. Heat the mixture through and pour this curry sauce over the chicken and cabbage just before serving.

Marinated Soya Fried Chicken   *Makes 6–8 pieces*

This method is similar to the one above, but uses a soya sauce marinade.

4 cloves garlic, finely chopped
2 tablespoons soya sauce
¼ teaspoon (1.25 ml) chilli sauce
1 tablespoon (15 ml) vegetable oil
6–8 chicken pieces (drumsticks are good)
plain flour for rolling the chicken in
oil for deep-frying

Combine the garlic, soya sauce, chilli sauce and oil and mix well together. Brush the chicken pieces with the mixture and leave them to marinate for 1 hour. Roll the chicken pieces in the flour and set aside. Heat the oil until it barely smokes and deep-fry the chicken (in batches if necessary) until golden brown and tender. Drain and serve.

Sweet and Sour Chicken   *Serves 4–6*

4 tablespoons (60 ml) vegetable oil
4 cloves garlic, finely chopped
approx. 3 lb (1.4 kg) frying chicken cut into pieces (see Cooks'
    Notes) *or* 4–6 joints chicken (legs, wings etc.) cut into pieces
4 fl oz (100 ml) white vinegar
4 oz (100 g) white sugar
2 tablespoons (30 ml) soya sauce
¼ teaspoon (1.25 ml) chilli sauce
1 teaspoon cornflour creamed in 1 tablespoon (15 ml) water
1 medium onion, chopped
1 green pepper, seeded and chopped
½ medium cucumber, peeled, seeded and chopped
2 medium tomatoes, blanched, peeled and chopped
4 oz (100 g) fresh *or* tinned pineapple chunks
salt to taste

Heat the oil in a wok or large saucepan and stir-fry the garlic until golden. Add the chicken pieces and fry them over a moderate heat, stirring often, until tender. During this time combine the vinegar, sugar, soya sauce, chilli sauce, and cornflour and water mixture in a small saucepan and set over a low heat. Stir the onion, pepper, cucumber, tomatoes and pineapple into the chicken and stir-fry for a little less than a minute after the addition of each one. Stir into the mixture the vinegar and sugar sauce and simmer over a low heat until the sauce thickens. Season to taste with salt, and serve.

Marinated Coriander Fried Chicken   *Makes 6–8 pieces*

This is one of those recipes that require coriander roots (see Cooks' Notes); however, it is worth the effort of finding some. Chicken pieces are rubbed with a garlic, coriander and pepper paste, left to marinate for an hour and then deep-fried. They are delicious as part of a buffet meal or served on their own with drinks.

8–10 cloves garlic
2 tablespoons coriander roots
1 tablespoon freshly ground black pepper
6–8 pieces of chicken (drumsticks are good)
oil for deep-frying

In a pestle and mortar grind the garlic, coriander roots and black pepper into a paste. Rub the paste over the chicken pieces and set them aside in the refrigerator for 1 hour. Heat the oil until it barely smokes and deep-fry the chicken pieces (in batches if necessary) until golden brown and tender. Drain and serve.

Variation

The chicken pieces may be barbecued instead of deep-fried.

Chicken Satay   *Serves 6–8*

Chicken pieces are marinated in a curry-flavoured mixture, then threaded onto skewers, grilled and served with a spicy, hot peanut sauce. Chicken Satay is a popular street food in Thailand. Serve it as a starter, part of a buffet, a snack, or with rice and Cucumber Salad Sauce (see Sauces) as a main course.

3 cloves garlic, finely chopped
2 teaspoons finely grated ginger root
1 tablespoon curry powder *or* a curry paste (see Curry Dishes)
1 teaspoon ground turmeric
1 teaspoon ground coriander
5 fl oz (125 ml) coconut milk *or* milk
4 chicken breasts about 2 lb (900 g) in weight, boned and cut
    into strips 1 in (2.5 cm) by ¼ in (0.75 cm)
peanut butter sauce (see Sauces)

Combine all the ingredients except the Peanut Butter Sauce in a mixing bowl or blender and beat well together. Put this marinade into a large bowl and add the chicken pieces. Baste each piece thoroughly with the marinade. Cover the bowl and set aside in the refrigerator for 2 hours or more. At the end of this time thread the chicken strips onto bamboo or metal skewers, leaving space at either end to hold the skewer. Pre-heat a hot grill or barbecue fire and grill the chicken close to the heat for 1–2 minutes each side. During this time sprinkle any leftover marinade over the Satay. During the grilling or barbecuing process aim to get the distance and heat just right, so that the finished Satay is speckled with dark brown singe marks. Serve with Peanut butter sauce in individual bowls. Dip the Chicken Satay in the sauce before eating.

Chicken in Coconut Sauce   *Serves 4*

approx. 3 lb (1.4 kg) frying chicken cut into pieces (see Cooks'
  Notes) *or* legs and thighs *or* four ½ breasts of chicken
1 pint (550 ml) medium coconut milk *or* 4 oz (100 g) creamed
  coconut dissolved in 16 fl oz (450 ml) hot water
5 peppercorns
2 teaspoons coriander seeds
1 red *or* green chilli, seeded
4 gloves garlic
2 teaspoons grated lemon rind *or* finely chopped lemon grass
2 tablespoons (30 ml) fish sauce
1 tablespoon roasted peanuts *or* smooth peanut butter

Garnish
finely chopped coriander leaves

Put the chicken into a saucepan and cover with the coconut milk.
Bring to a gentle boil and simmer, uncovered, for 30 minutes.
Meanwhile, in an electric blender or pestle and mortar, grind the
peppercorns and coriander seeds, then add the chilli, garlic,
lemon rind, fish sauce and peanuts and grind to a smooth paste.
Add a little of the coconut milk from the chicken pot to dilute the
paste, and then pour it onto the chicken. Stir well, return the pot
to the boil and simmer until the chicken is tender (another 10–15
minutes). Serve garnished with coriander leaves.

Note: By the end of the cooking period the sauce should have
been reduced to less than half its original volume. If the chicken is
tender before the sauce is thick enough, lift it out with a slotted
spoon, keep it warm in a hot oven and reduce the remaining sauce
over a medium heat. If the opposite happens and the cooking
liquid reduces too quickly, cover the pan during the latter half of
the cooking period.

Won-ton Chicken   *Serves 6*

This dish is essentially a chicken soup with minced pork-filled
won-ton. It is, however, a substantial meal – a main course dish
rather than a soup. The ingredients call for won-ton skins,
paper-thin circles of pastry dough available ready-made at any
Chinese grocery store.

Soup

2 tablespoons (30 ml) vegetable oil
2 cloves garlic, crushed
1 lb (450 g) chicken pieces (legs, thighs etc.) cut into 6 portions
1 teaspoon ground coriander
½ teaspoon ground black pepper
¼ teaspoon ground cloves
½ teaspoon ground ginger
2 tablespoons (30 ml) soya sauce
1¼ pints (750 ml) water *or* stock
6 dried Chinese mushrooms soaked for 30 minutes in hot water,
   drained, stems discarded (optional)

Won-ton

4 oz (100 g) finely minced pork
1 clove garlic, finely chopped
¼ teaspoon salt
¼ teaspoon black pepper
20 won-ton skins

Greens

4 oz (100 g) Chinese greens or spinach, finely chopped

Heat the oil in a large saucepan and stir-fry the garlic until golden.
Add the chicken pieces and lightly brown them on both sides.
Add the remaining soup ingredients, stir well, bring to the boil,
reduce the heat, cover and simmer for 50 minutes or until the
chicken is tender. Meanwhile make the won-ton. Combine the
pork with the garlic, salt and pepper and mix well together. Place
about 1 teaspoon of the mixture in the centre of each won-ton
skin. Fold the filled won-ton skins into half-moon shapes and seal
them, then turn the two corners in and press them flat to seal
them. Cook the won-ton by lowering them into a pan of gently
boiling water for 3–4 minutes. Drain them, sprinkle with a little
oil to stop them sticking together, and set aside. Just before the
soup is finished blanch the greens or spinach in boiling water for
3 minutes. Drain. To present the Won-ton Chicken, divide the
greens and won-ton among six bowls. Put a piece of chicken and
one mushroom (if used) in each bowl, and then divide the soup
stock among them. Serve immediately.

Chicken and Spinach in Peanut Sauce   *Serves 4*

1 teaspoon ground ginger
2 cloves garlic, finely chopped
3 tablespoons (45 ml) vegetable oil
1 teaspoon curry powder
1 tablespoon (15 ml) single cream
2 chicken breasts, boned and cut into ¼ in (0.75 cm) thick slices
2 tablespoons finely diced onion
1 red chilli, seeded and finely chopped
2 tablespoons peanut butter
2 teaspoons (10 ml) fish sauce *or* soya sauce
2 teaspoons sugar
4 fl oz (100 ml) coconut milk *or* milk
10 oz (300 g) spinach, cleaned, drained and chopped

Combine the ginger, garlic, 1½ tablespoons (25 ml) vegetable oil, curry powder and cream in a bowl and mix well together. Add the chicken slices and make sure each piece is coated with the mixture. Cover and set aside in the refrigerator for 1 hour or more. Boil a pan of water ready to blanch the spinach. Heat the remaining oil in a wok or saucepan and stir-fry the onion until golden brown. Reduce the heat and stir in the chilli, peanut butter, fish sauce, sugar and coconut milk. Stir well and set on a very low simmer. Put the chicken pieces and marinade into another saucepan and stir-fry them until lightly browned and tender. Remove from the heat. Blanch the spinach in boiling water until wilted. Drain, and make a bed of spinach on a serving plate. Pour the chicken on top, and over the chicken pour the peanut sauce. Serve immediately.

Eggs-Tra!

7 June 1985. My birthday. I am happy. I have survived the latter half of 1984 without Orwellian vicissitudes, have completed nearly half of 1985 similarly unscathed.

Anong and the monkeys extend birthday greetings. I open the daily newspaper. The lead story, boring, boring news about boring politicians and a boring, boring parliamentary censure debate. Beneath, however, a shorter news item almost leaps off the page. Local police have arrested a thirty-three-year-old woman for claiming to have laid two eggs.

But, ahah, there's *more*. The woman was arrested for *public fraud* after a doctor identified 'her' eggs as boiled duck eggs she could not possibly have delivered (!) She, reportedly pregnant for ten months and nine days, dreamed of talking with two children dressed in white. The said children claimed they wanted to stay with the woman. Later that evening, purportedly, she delivered the two eggs. Thereafter, according to the police, several local people visited the woman and her husband to donate money and pay their respects.

The item triggers eggs-oteric thoughts that something like this could occur only in Bangkok, the Orient's most eggs-otic city. We could digress and describe the capital's egg-citing nocturnal attractions when eggs-travagant eggs-penditures are often egg-acted for eggs-plicit services. However. . . . Eggs-clusively concerning eggs, there are *Kai Yiiaow Ma*, 'Horse Urine Eggs', an hors d'oeuvre sold as 'Thousand-Year-Old Eggs' and formerly prepared by burying chickens' eggs and . . . no, we won't eggs-trapolate.

Moreover, the Thai word for egg, *Kai*, shares the same slang meaning as 'jewels' and 'nuts' in English, which makes it devilish difficult to know if someone talking about his eggs actually means his eggs, or his eggs.

Elsewhere, David Scott offers the origin of 'Son-in-Law's Eggs'.

Could there, possibly, be another?

Curry Dishes

Green curry paste•Red curry paste•Orange curry paste•
Massaman (Muslim) curry paste•Mild curry paste•Massaman
curry (Thai Muslim beef curry•Curried pork with vegetables•
Green Beef curry•Red prawn or shrimp curry•Chicken curry•
Dry chicken or beef curry•Fried curried rice•Fried curried
noodles•Fish and vegetable curry

Thai curry pastes are made from distinctive mixtures of herbs and
spices. They are distinguished from one another by their colours.
The hottest is Green curry paste, which contains a mouth-
numbing quantity of fresh green chillies, seeds and all. The pastes
are listed above in decreasing order of hotness. I have also included
a recipe for a Mild curry paste, for those people who do not like
very hot food. It may be substituted for any of the curry pastes
given in the recipes to ensure that a dish is only mildly flavoured.

Curry pastes usually contain quite a lot of ingredients, but are all
quick and simple to prepare, especially if you have an electric blender.
Experiment and adjust the quantities to suit your tastes. Reduce the
quantities of chillies used if you do not like fiery food. All the recipes
may be halved or doubled, etc. to make more or less of a particular
paste. To save time you may substitute a curry powder paste: 2
tablespoons of powder mixed with two tablespoons (30 ml) white
vinegar and the same quantity of water.

Massaman (Muslim) Curry Paste
Makes 6–8 tablespoons (90–120 ml)

Massaman is the mildest of genuine Thai curry pastes. The word
is a Thai corruption of 'Muslim' and this paste reflects the
influence of Indian tastes. It contains cinnamon, cloves and
nutmeg, spices not normally used in Thai cooking. Massaman
curries, because of their mildness, are usually the most acceptable
to foreigners in Thailand.

1 tablespoon ground coriander
2 teaspoons ground caraway
½ teaspoon ground cardamom
½ teaspoon ground cinnamon
½ teaspoon ground cloves
1 teaspoon ground ginger
2 teaspoons grated lemon rind *or* finely chopped lemon grass
3 tablespoons (45 ml) vegetable oil
2–4 dried red chillies, seeded, soaked in warm water for 10–15
   minutes, drained and chopped *or* 1 tablespoon chilli powder
4 cloves garlic, crushed
1 medium onion, chopped
½ teaspoon shrimp paste *or* anchovy paste (optional)

In a small bowl mix together the coriander, caraway, cardamom, cinnamon, cloves, ginger, chilli powder (if used) and lemon rind. Set aside. Heat the oil in a frying pan and sauté the drained chillies (if used), garlic and onion until the onion is softened. Transfer the mixture to a blender. Add the shrimp paste, if used, and the spice mixture and blend to a smooth paste. Store unused paste in a screw-top jar in the refrigerator, where it will keep for up to a month.

Red Curry Paste   *Makes 6–8 tablespoons (90–120 ml)*

Like the Green curry paste, this paste is very hot. For a milder flavour reduce the number of red chillies. Store unused paste in a screw-top jar in the refrigerator, where it will keep for 5–6 weeks.

12–14 medium dried red chillies, seeded and soaked in warm
   water for 10–15 minutes, then drained
2 teaspoons ground caraway
2 teaspoons ground coriander
½ teaspoon ground ginger
1 teaspoon freshly ground black pepper
4 cloves garlic, chopped
2 teaspoons grated lemon rind *or* finely chopped lemon grass
½ medium onion *or* 2 shallots, chopped
1 tablespoon finely chopped coriander roots
1 teaspoon salt
1 tablespoon shrimp paste *or* anchovy paste
4 tablespoons (60 ml) vegetable oil

Put all the ingredients into a blender and blend to a smooth paste. Use as required.

Orange Curry Paste   *Makes 4 tablespoons (60 ml)*

This paste is basically pounded chilli peppers flavoured with shrimp paste and a little onion, and soured with a small amount of vinegar. It is used in seafood dishes.

10 dried red chillies, seeded and soaked in warm water
   for 10–15 minutes, then drained.
1 teaspoon salt
2 tablespoons finely chopped onion *or* shallot
1 tablespoon shrimp paste *or* anchovy paste
1 teaspoon (5 ml) rice vinegar *or* cider vinegar

Drain the chillies and chop them finely. In a pestle and mortar pound the chillies with the salt. Add the onion and continue pounding until well pulverized. Add the shrimp paste and vinegar and pound the mixture to a smooth paste. A blender may be used in place of the pestle and mortar, but it doesn't bring out the flavours of the ingredients in the same way.

Green Curry Paste   *Makes 6–8 tablespoons (90–120 ml)*

This paste is extremely hot. For a milder curry, reduce the number of green chillies. Store unused paste in a small screw-top jar in the refrigerator, where it will keep for 5–6 weeks.

8 whole green chillies with seeds
1 teaspoon ground coriander
1 teaspoon ground caraway
1 teaspoon freshly ground black pepper
½ teaspoon ground ginger
1 teaspoon salt
1 teaspoon ground nutmeg
2 teaspoons grated lemon rind *or* finely chopped lemon grass
2 tablespoons finely chopped shallot *or* onion
1 tablespoon coriander roots, finely chopped
4 cloves garlic, finely chopped
1 teaspoon shrimp paste *or* anchovy paste
4 tablespoons (60 ml) vegetable oil

Put all the ingredients except the shrimp paste and vegetable oil into a small, dry frying pan over a medium heat and stir-fry for 3 to 4 minutes. Transfer the mixture to a blender (or a pestle and mortar) and add the shrimp paste and oil. Blend or pound to a smooth paste.

Mild Curry Paste   *Makes 5–6 tablespoons (75–90 ml)*

1 tablespoon ground caraway
1 tablespoon ground coriander
¼–½ teaspoon chilli powder *or* chilli sauce
1 teaspoon freshly ground black pepper
1 teaspoon ground turmeric
2 tablespoons shrimp paste *or* anchovy paste
2 teaspoons (10 ml) rice vinegar *or* cider vinegar

Stir together the dry ingredients. Stir the mixture into the shrimp paste and vinegar, and mix well. Store unused paste in a small screw-top jar in the refrigerator, where it will keep for up to one month.

Massaman Curry (Thai Muslim Beef Curry) *Serves 4–6*

Serve over rice.

1½ lb (700 g) stewing beef, trimmed and cut into 1 in (2.5 cm) cubes
1¼ pints (750 ml) thick coconut milk *or* 5 oz (125 g) creamed coconut dissolved in 1 pint (550 ml) boiling water
1 tablespoon (15 ml) fish sauce
4 oz (100 g) roasted unsalted peanuts
2 tablespoons (30 ml) lemon *or* lime juice
1 oz (25 g) tamarind *or* 2 more tablespoons (30 ml) lemon *or* lime juice
2–3 tablespoons Massaman curry paste
sugar to taste

Bring the beef and coconut milk to the boil in a saucepan, stirring continuously. Add the fish sauce and peanuts and reduce the heat to very low. Simmer uncovered until the beef is tender; depending on the quality of the beef, about 1–1½ hours. Meanwhile, if you are using tamarind soak it in 2 fl oz (50 ml) boiling water for 15 minutes and then bring to the boil. Simmer for 5 minutes and strain the mixture through a sieve. Press the last of the liquid from the pulp with the back of a spoon and then discard it. Reserve the tamarind water. Remove the beef from the saucepan using a slotted spoon and set it aside on a plate. Reduce the cooking liquid by one-third over a high heat. Stir the curry paste into the cooking liquid and return the meat to the pan. Stir in the tamarind water and/or lemon or lime juice, add sugar to taste, bring to the boil and serve.

Curried Pork with Vegetables   *Serves 4*

The vegetables given here are only suggestions, and any suitable combination you have available may be used. This curry, unlike most Thai curries, does not use coconut milk and it is a little quicker to prepare. Serve with rice.

3 tablespoons (45 ml) vegetable oil
2 tablespoons Red *or* Green curry paste
8 oz (225 g) pork fillet cut into thin strips
2 tablespoons (30 ml) fish sauce
1 teaspoon grated lemon rind *or* chopped lemon grass
4 oz (100 g) green beans, cut into 2 in (5 cm) lengths
4 oz (100 g) cauliflower, cut into florets
4 oz (100 g) cabbage *or* Chinese cabbage, coarsely shredded
4 oz (100 g) fresh mushrooms, sliced
2 teaspoons sugar

Garnish

finely chopped coriander *or* mint *or* parsley leaves

Heat the oil in a large pan or wok and stir-fry the curry paste for 3–4 minutes. Add the pork, fish sauce and lemon rind and continue to stir-fry for a further 6–7 minutes. Add the green beans, cauliflower, cabbage and mushrooms. Cook, stirring, until they are tender enough to eat but still retain some 'bite' (about 4–5 minutes). Stir in the sugar and serve garnished with fresh herbs.

Green Beef Curry   *Serves 4–6*

Serve over rice.

3 tablespoons (45 ml) vegetable oil
3 tablespoons Green curry paste
1½ lb (700 g) lean beef cut into ½ in (1.25 cm) by 2 in (5 cm) slices
1¼ pints (750 ml) thick coconut milk *or* 5 oz (125 g) creamed coconut dissolved in 1 pint (550 ml) boiling water
2 tablespoons (30 ml) fish sauce
2 teaspoons sugar
1 green chilli, seeded and chopped (optional)
1 teaspoon grated lemon rind

Garnish

finely chopped coriander leaves

Heat the oil in a large pan or wok and stir-fry the curry paste over a moderate heat for 3–4 minutes. Add the beef and stir-fry for a further 3–4 minutes. Pour in the coconut milk and bring to a slow boil, stirring all the time. Stir in the fish sauce and sugar, and simmer over a low heat until the beef is tender (30–40 minutes). Stir in the chilli pepper, if used, and lemon rind. Simmer for a further 3 minutes and serve garnished with coriander leaves.

Red Prawn or Shrimp Curry   *Serves 4*

This is a very hot curry. Use the Mild curry paste if you are not used to fiery food.

2 tablespoons (30 ml) vegetable oil
8 oz (225 g) shelled prawns *or* shrimps (about 1½ lb (700 g)
   unshelled prawns or shrimps)
1 medium onion sliced
2 tablespoons Red *or* Mild curry paste
½ pint (275 ml) thick coconut milk *or* 3 oz (75 g) creamed
   coconut dissolved in 8 fl oz (225 ml) boiling water
1 tablespoon (15 ml) lemon juice
1 tablespoon sugar
salt and black pepper to taste

Garnish
finely chopped coriander leaves

Heat the oil in a pan or wok and add the prawns. Stir-fry for a minute or two until they turn pink. Remove the prawns with a slotted spoon and set aside. Add the onion and fry until softened. Add the curry paste to the pan and stir-fry over a low heat for 3–4 minutes. Add the coconut milk and bring to a slow boil, stirring continuously. Add the lemon juice, sugar, and salt and black pepper to taste. Put the prawns back into the pan, add the onions and simmer for 10 minutes. Serve garnished with coriander leaves.

Variation
Replace the onion with 1 large cucumber, peeled, seeded and cubed.

Chicken Curry   *Serves 6*

Serve over rice.

3 tablespoons (45 ml) vegetable oil
3–4 lb (1.4–1.8 kg) frying chicken skinned and cut into serving
  pieces (see Cooks' Notes)
2 cloves garlic, crushed
1 medium onion, chopped
2 tablespoons Green *or* Mild curry paste
1½ pints (900 ml) thick coconut milk *or* 6 oz (175 g) creamed
  coconut dissolved in 1¼ pints (750 ml) boiling water
1 tablespoon dried sweet basil
1 teaspoon grated lemon rind
4 oz (100 g) fresh *or* frozen *or* tinned green peas

Heat the oil in a large saucepan or wok and brown the chicken
pieces. Remove them and set aside on a plate. Add the garlic and
onion to the pan and stir-fry until the onion is softened. Stir in the
curry paste and stir-fry for 2–3 minutes. Put the chicken back into
the pan and coat each piece with curry paste. Pour in the coconut
milk, add the basil and lemon rind and bring to the boil, stirring
continuously. Reduce the heat and simmer uncovered until the
chicken is tender (about 50 minutes). Add a little milk, water or
stock if the cooking liquid reduces too much during the
simmering period. Ten minutes before the end of the cooking
time, add the peas to the pan. Serve as soon as the chicken is
tender.

Variation

Substitute chicken stock for the coconut milk, and stir in 8 fl oz
(225 ml) single cream just before you serve the curry.

Dry Chicken or Beef Curry   *Serves 4*

This is a thick, delicious curry usually made with Red curry
paste. However, it is also good with Mild curry paste.
Aubergines or courgettes are sometimes added as well. Serve
over rice.

2 tablespoons (30 ml) vegetable oil
1 lb (450 g) lean beef *or* chicken meat cut into slices ½ in
  (2.5 cm) by 2 in (5 cm)
3 tablespoons Red *or* Mild curry paste
8 fl oz (225 ml) thick coconut milk *or* 3 oz (75 g) creamed
  coconut, dissolved in 8 fl oz (225 ml) boiling water

2 tablespoons coarsely ground roasted peanuts *or*
  crunchy peanut butter
2 tablespoons (30 ml) fish sauce
1 tablespoon sugar
1 lb (450 g) aubergines, cut into bite-size pieces, salted,
  pressed and rinsed (optional)

Garnish
fresh basil, coriander or parsley

Heat the oil in a wok or large frying pan and stir-fry the chicken
or beef until nicely browned and partially cooked. Remove the
meat from the wok or pan with a slotted spoon and set aside on a
plate. In the remaining oil stir-fry the curry paste over a low heat
for 2–3 minutes. Add the coconut milk, stir well and bring to a
slow boil, stirring continuously. Add the peanuts, fish sauce and
sugar and mix well. Return the meat to the pan and continue to
cook over a low heat until the meat is tender (about 20 minutes).
If you are using aubergines add them 5 minutes after the meat has
been returned to the pan.

Fried Curried Rice   *Serves 4*

3 tablespoons (45 ml) vegetable oil
1–2 tablespoons Massaman *or* Mild curry paste
8 oz (225 g) bean curd, drained, pressed and cut into 1 in
  (2.5 cm) cubes
8 oz (225 g) green beans, cut into 1 in (2.5 cm) lengths and
  blanched just tender in boiling water, then drained
2 lb (900 g) cooked long grain rice (about 12 oz/350 g) raw rice)
2 tablespoons finely chopped onion *or* shallot
2 spring onions, finely chopped
1–2 red chillies, seeded and finely chopped (optional)
1 tablespoon (15 ml) lemon *or* lime juice
1 tablespoon (15 ml) soya sauce

Heat the oil in a wok or large frying pan and stir-fry the curry
paste for 3–4 minutes. Add the bean curd and beans and stir-fry
until well heated through. Add the rice, mix well and continue to
stir-fry until heated through. Transfer to a serving dish or bowl.
Over the top, sprinkle chopped onions and spring onions, and
chillies (if used). Finally sprinkle with lemon juice and soya sauce
and serve.

Fried Curried Noodles

Replace the cooked rice in the recipe above with cooked, drained egg noodles.

Fish and Vegetable Curry *Serves 4*

Almost any type of filleted fish may be used in this curry, and whatever combination of vegetables you like. The method is simple and does not use coconut milk. For a hot curry use Orange curry paste, and for a milder one Mild curry paste.

2 tablespoons (30 ml) vegetable oil
2 cloves garlic, crushed
½ medium onion, finely chopped
1 lb (450 g) filleted fish, cut into large bite-size pieces
½ pint (275 ml) water *or* stock
2 tablespoons Orange *or* Milk curry paste
2 tablespoons (30 ml) lemon juice
2 tablespoons (30 ml) fish sauce
1 lb (450 g) vegetables, e.g.:

green beans, cut into 2 in (5 cm) lengths
cauliflower, cut into florets
Chinese cabbage, coarsely shredded
fresh mushrooms, sliced
tinned bamboo shoots, sliced

Garnish
finely chopped coriander leaves

Heat the oil in a saucepan or wok and sauté the garlic and onion until golden. Add the fish and water and bring to the boil. Reduce the heat and simmer, uncovered, for 7–8 minutes. With a slotted spoon lift out about one-third of the fish chunks and transfer them to the goblet of a blender. Add 4 fl oz (100 ml) of liquid from the pan, the curry paste, lemon juice and fish sauce. Blend until smooth and return the mixture to the pan. Add the vegetables to the pan, leaving those with a short cooking time to the last, and simmer uncovered until they are tender (about 10 minutes). Garnish with coriander leaves and serve.

The Human Touch

In the late afternoons and early evenings, the satisfying rhythmic sounds of granite striking granite emanate from built-up residential areas as, concealed within kitchens, women use pestles and mortars to pound together spices and herbs that flavour, enrich and enliven the evening meal.

In a country where tradition dies hard (if ever), pestles and mortars are still favoured over electric blenders, the latter's availability and acknowledged convenience notwithstanding. The preference extends both to private homes and restaurants, thankfully numerous, where traditional culinary skills have not been sacrificed for speed, nor spicy cuisine usurped by bland concoctions.

Anong explains the preference in simple terms. 'Blenders are too crude.'

'How so?'

'You can't be subtle with them.'

'Mortars and pestles are *subtle*?' I reply, thinking of the perpetual rhythm that can give otherwise lovely women overdeveloped biceps.

'Sure. You can add, alter, change, adjust whatever you are mixing. You can never match that precise control with a blender.'

'That's all?'

'Well . . . blenders lack the human touch.'

'Now you're talking. Are mortars and pestles used for anything else besides mashing spices?'

'For blending traditional medicines.'

'And?'

'Older country women use them for preparing betel.'

'Anything else?'

'Thai women have always used pestles for hitting the heads of errant husbands.'

'Why use a pestle?'

'You can't inflict sufficient damage with a blender.'

Score two for tradition.

Sauces

Hot fish sauce (*Nam Prik*)•Vietnamese fish sauce•Sweet and hot
fish sauce•Cucumber salad sauce•Sweet and sour
sauce•Peanut butter sauce

Nam Pla, Thai fish sauce, is the basis of many Thai dishes and of
Nam Prik, the chilli hot sauces served with every Thai meal. *Nam
Pla* is available at any Oriental food store under the name fish
sauce. *Nam Prik* is the general name for hot sauce, and also the
specific name for the most popular version of *Nam Prik*. This is
made from dried salted fish, fish sauce, garlic, chillies and lime
juice or lemon juice, all pounded together. *Nam Prik* is a must at
any Thai meal, be it a simple lunch or an elaborate dinner. Serve
these sauces as accompaniments to main dishes or for the specific
purposes described in the recipes.

Hot Fish Sauce (*Nam Prik*)   *Makes 3 fl oz (75 ml)*

This is a stronger-tasting, more fiery version of the regular *Nam
Pla*. Hot fish sauce will pep up the taste of almost any dish for
those who like strongly flavoured food.

1 tablespoon (15 ml) fish sauce
4 anchovy fillets *or* 2 tablespoons of other salted fish, flaked or
  chopped dried shrimps
3 tablespoons (45 ml) lemon *or* lime juice
4–6 cloves garlic
1 tablespoon (15 ml) soya sauce
1 teaspoon sugar
½–2 (according to taste) fresh red or green chillies, seeded
  and finely chopped

Put all the ingredients into a blender and blend to a smooth paste,
or use a pestle and mortar and pound them together.

Variation
For a milder sauce add water to taste.

Vietnamese Fish Sauce　　　*Makes 4 fl oz (100 ml)*

A milder variation of the hot fish sauce above, Vietnamese in origin but also popular in Thailand.

5 tablespoons (75 ml) fish sauce
2 tablespoons (30 ml) lemon *or* lime juice
2 tablespoons (30 ml) water
3 cloves garlic, crushed
1 teaspoon sugar
Hot pepper or chilli sauce to taste (optional)

Put all the ingredients through a blender or just whisk them together in a bowl.

Sweet and Hot Fish Sauce   *Makes enough for 8 people*

Serve with plain rice, vegetables, salads, chicken or fish dishes.

1 tablespoon (15 ml) vegetable oil
1 medium onion, finely chopped
4 cloves garlic, finely chopped
½–1 dried red chilli, seeded and finely chopped
1 tablespoon dark brown sugar
2 tablespoons (30 ml) lemon juice *or* tamarind water
4 tablespoons (60 ml) fish sauce
2 spring onions, finely chopped
2 tablespoons finely chopped coriander leaves

Heat the oil in a small pan and stir-fry the onion and garlic until golden. Add the chilli and stir-fry for 1 minute. Remove from the heat and transfer to a serving bowl. In the same pan heat the sugar, lemon juice and fish sauce and bring to a slow boil. Stir in the spring onions and coriander leaves and pour the mixture into the serving bowl with the onion mixture. Mix well, set aside to cool to room temperature, and serve.

Cucumber Salad Sauce   *Serves 4*

More a salad than a sauce, but served over chilli hot dishes it is cooling and refreshing.

1 tablespoon (15 ml) cider vinegar *or* rice vinegar
2 tablespoons sugar
2 tablespoons (30 ml) hot water
½ teaspoon salt
½ medium cucumber, thinly sliced
½ small onion, thinly sliced
1 red chilli, seeded and finely chopped

Put the vinegar, sugar, hot water and salt into a small bowl and stir until the sugar dissolves completely. Arrange the cucumber slices on a serving dish and pour over them the vinegar mixture. Decorate the top with onion slices, garnish with chilli pepper, chill and serve.

Sweet and Sour Sauce   *Makes 7 fl oz (200 ml)*

Serve in the usual way with meat or fish dishes. Also served over sliced cucumber as an accompaniment to Satay.

4 fl oz (100 ml) water
2 tablespoons cornflour paste
2 fl oz (50 ml) white vinegar
2 tablespoons sugar
1 tablespoon tomato purée
salt to taste

Heat the water in a small pan, then cream the cornflour with 1 tablespoon (15 ml) of the water when it is hot. Stir the paste back into the pan and add the other ingredients. Stir continuously over a low heat until the mixture thickens. Transfer the sauce to a bowl, allow to cool and serve.

Peanut Butter Sauce   *Makes ½ pint (275 ml)*

Peanut butter sauce usually accompanies Satay dishes, but it is also good as a dipping sauce with raw vegetables or as a side dish with meat or chicken dishes.

8 fl oz (225 ml) medium coconut milk *or* 2 oz (50 g) creamed
    coconut dissolved in 6 fl oz (175 ml) hot water
1 tablespoon Massaman Curry Paste
2 tablespoons smooth peanut butter
1 tablespoon sugar
1 tablespoon (15 ml) lemon juice
1 tablespoon (15 ml) fish sauce *or* soya sauce
salt to taste

Heat the coconut milk in a saucepan over a low heat. Stir in the curry paste and then the other ingredients. Stirring continuously, bring to the boil. Reduce the heat and simmer, uncovered, for 5 minutes. Serve.

Note: Curry paste of your own preparation may be substituted for the Massaman curry paste.

Grabbits

Anong keeps a brown rabbit on her kitchen floor among earthenware jars containing fermented fish. Whenever she needs to grate dried coconuts for sweets or desserts or curries she drags her rabbit out, sits on it and noisily grates her coconuts on the rabbit's head.

Precisely why the wooden and iron contraption should be called a *Katai Koot Mapraow* ('coconut-grating rabbit') defies logic and cannot be satisfactorily explained – 'The contraption resembles a rabbit,' (it does not); 'The spiky head resembles rabbit's teeth' (it does not) etc. – by Thai friends who range from advertising executives and restaurateurs to Buddhist monks and poets.

My insistent pursuit of *why* the contraption is so called irritates Anong, who claims that her rabbit has two hundred uses and gets uncharacteristically shirty when asked to define them.

The whole business has almost driven me out of my skull. A coconut-grating rabbit! It's damn nearly as unreasonable a name as a clothes-horse.

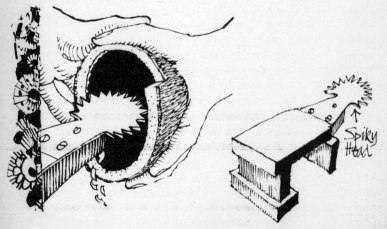

Midsummer Mango Madness

Thai fruits are so abundant and varied that someone could easily write a book about them. Some, such as bananas (of which there are some twenty edible varieties), oranges and papayas are available throughout the year. Others, including the spiky, creamy durian and hairy rambutan, are seasonal. Each fruit has its enthusiasts, though probably none inspires more passion, poetry and midsummer madness than mangoes, arguably the most luscious tropical fruits of all.

Thailand's mango season coincides with the hot season, a humid, enervating three-month period from March through May, made partly bearable by brisk winds.

Local mangoes (more than twenty different varieties) are the major ingredients of numerous desserts, chutneys, jams and confectionery, and have flesh ranging from a crisp pale green to a pulpy bright orange. Their ambrosial tastes range from the sweet to the indescribably subtle.

To the uninitiated, all mango trees look alike, but local mango connoisseurs (25 million Thai women) can distinguish them at a glance or whiff. We have two mango trees, each taller than the house. One produces long, slim fruits that beguile the palate. The other produces a stubby mango that is popularly eaten before it ripens fully. Crisp and crunchy, it is enjoyed like a sliced apple, often with a dip made from dried prawns, shredded onions, shrimp paste, dried chillies and sugared fish sauce.

From blossom time onwards, both trees are subject to daily inspection for parasites, leaf damage and fungus. Come the momentous day when tiny fruits appear, the trees become central to Anong's increasingly euphoric existence. Euphoria escalates daily as mangoes mature.

Each morning, Anong counts them like a miser gloating over a secret hoard. The trees' condition becomes an accurate emotional barometer – increasing fruit tallies guarantee radiant smiles, loving looks and open-hearted generosity, whereas a fallen fruit fashions scowls, Teutonic brooding and deeply furrowed brows.

Nascent paranoia festers once squirrels pay attention to the ripening fruit. Then Anong regards them as devils incarnate: they become invested with the ugliest, most evil, most obscene motives. Annual hatred commences when they nibble ripening mangoes. Despoiled fruit tumbles to the ground, to be discovered during daily inspections. Anong will bring spoilt fruit to the kitchen where, chances are, I'm innocently drinking coffee, scanning the daily rag.

She'll thrust spoilt mangoes under my nose and unleash impassioned invective. My conversational Thai is adequate for everyday conversation but deficient for understanding her annual tirades against mango-spoiling squirrels. Choice multi-syllable expletives and vitriolic assault merely bewilder.

'Look at what those flakaflitpeckjungtitat squirrels did to this pernoscatacufagafugsamnitanatit mango! If I had a cascuspace-fugkluaypitapat gun I'd greffanafagafugtatiwongwangsirmonkanutatana every gunganagunganthackatit squirrel in gagasat sight!'

'Pardon?'

'I parasantajungrararakjungratitatat said. . . .'

'Calm down.'

'Papasakarakasarajakatanwong calm down karachatakawang when wongwangwungjungsakatit squirrels lunawong-chuwee. . . .'

'Jesus Christ. . . .'

'Tikhayayanamahatattitarai Jesus perfluggatawangwong. . . .'

Once calmed, she has to be dissuaded from organizing vigilantes to stand guard over neighbourhood trees.

One might reasonably assume that emotional identification with two mango trees would suffice.

Never.

Frequently I'll be driving, Anong beside me, the monkeys in the back. Every tenth driver is suicidal; jaywalkers appear without warning; buses hog the centre of the road; taxis signal right turns before turning left. I'll be totally absorbed in the thunderous madness surrounding us when Anong will emit an excited shriek that never fails to startle and frighten me. The shriek precedes praise for a briefly glimpsed mango tree, laden with fruit, in someone's garden. The monkeys will respond with similar enthusiasm, whereupon the car becomes a travelling farmyard complete with effusive brays, whistles, hoots, howls, barks, coos, snorts, squeals, moos, neighs, bellows, yelps, screeches, chuckles, whoops, grunts, miaows and gobbling sounds that signify the extent to which successive mango trees excite my family's imagination. *Every* mango tree elicits comment. The emotional dam has burst.

Eating mangoes, obviously, is the greatest pleasure. But nothing's more pleasurable than eating mangoes you've picked yourself. I doubt if Thai women are ever happier than when they have a basket, a mango tree groaning with fruit and a long pole with a baffled cane trap for plucking ripe fruit. Barring such equipment, a ladder will suffice.

I've long stopped watching Anong climb our mango trees. Both are alive with nomadic red ants, vicious little beggars that bite painfully, tree snakes, various birds, butterflies, spiders and squirrels. Anong clambers like a reckless monkey, slapping off ants from her hands and ankles, balancing on frail branches that ordinarily wouldn't support a sparrow, in order to pluck mangoes from the trees' extremities.

Her basket filled, she'll happily descend, particularly if she hasn't discovered further evidence of squirrel vandalism, and transfer the mangoes to the refrigerator. Throughout the season, our refrigerator will groan with mangoes. When Anong is out, I will replace them with beer. When I am out, she will replace the beer with mangoes.

Verily, there are times when I wish I could sleep through the bloody mango season.

Mangoes dwindle by the time cooling rains herald the rains season in late May and early June. Spiky durians have come and gone. Mangosteens and rambutans make their appearance. The squirrels regain their entertaining characters for the remainder of the year.

A sense of calm prevails.

Desserts

Baked coconut custard•Sticky rice with mangoes•Shallow-fried bananas•Coconut pancakes•Deep-fried bananas•Bananas in coconut milk•Baked ginger and citrus bananas

A Thai meal can be concluded with either a basket of fresh fruit or sweet desserts, or even, in some cases, both. Thai cuisine has a varied repertoire of sweet dishes and sweetmeats which are often enjoyed as between-meal snacks and treats. They are often bought ready-made in the markets, or from roadside vendors, or served in restaurants. They usually contain ingredients uncommon in the West such as the fruits taro or yam, mangoes, lychis, custard apple, jackfruit and the exotic and expensive durian, or the cake ingredients lotus seeds, mung bean paste, agar-agar, palm sugar, cassava roots and tapioca flour. For this section I have selected just a few Thai sweet dishes that can be prepared in a Western kitchen. They all contain one or more of the most common Thai sweet ingredients, coconut, coconut milk (see Cooks' Notes for simple preparation) and bananas.

Baked Coconut Custard   *Serves 4–6*

8 fl oz (225 ml) medium coconut milk
4 eggs beaten
4 oz (100 g) light brown sugar
pinch of salt

Pre-heat the oven to 350° F (180° C, gas mark 4). Whisk together all the ingredients in a saucepan over a moderate heat and cook, stirring continuously, until the mixture starts to thicken (about 7–8 minutes). Lightly grease a 9 in (22.5 cm) diameter flan or pie dish and pour in the mixture. Bake for 30 minutes or until the top is lightly browned. Allow to cool before cutting into portions.

Variation

In Thailand the coconut custard is steamed inside a hollowed-out coconut shell. Instead of pouring the custard mixture into a pie dish, pour it into a coconut shell with the top cut off and the meat scraped out. Place the coconut shell on a plate on an upturned bowl in a pan with 1 in (2.5 cm) water in it, and steam for 30–40 minutes or until the custard is set. Chill and serve.

Sticky Rice with Mangoes   *Serves 4–6*

This dessert is everyone's favourite during the mango season. If glutinous rice is unavailable, short grain pudding rice may be substituted.

10 fl oz (275 ml) medium coconut milk
2 oz (50 g) white sugar
½ teaspoon salt
10 oz (275 g) glutinous (sticky) rice, soaked overnight, drained and cooked
4 ripe mangoes, peeled, halved, stones removed and sliced crosswise

In a large bowl mix together 8 fl oz (225 ml) of the coconut milk, the sugar and salt, and stir until the sugar dissolves. Stir in the still warm cooked rice, cover, and set aside for 20–30 minutes. Meanwhile simmer the remaining coconut milk in a small pan, uncovered, for 10 minutes. Place the sticky rice in the centre of a serving plate, arrange the mango slices around it, sprinkle the rice with the simmered coconut milk and serve.

Shallow-Fried Bananas   *Serves 4*

2 tablespoons (30 ml) peanut oil *or* butter
4 firm bananas, peeled, sliced lengthwise and then crosswise to give 4 pieces per banana
3 tablespoons brown *or* white sugar (according to taste)
lemon *or* lime juice to taste

Heat the oil or butter in a wok or frying pan. Add the banana pieces and fry them on both sides over a moderate heat until very lightly browned. Spoon over them the sugar, and gently stir it in until it dissolves. Transfer the bananas and sugar syrup to serving dishes, sprinkle with lemon or lime juice and serve.

Coconut Pancakes   *Makes 12 pancakes*

1 pint (550 ml) thin coconut milk *or* 4 oz (100 g) creamed coconut
    blended with 16 fl oz (450 ml) water
3 eggs, beaten
5 oz (150 g) rice flour *or* plain white flour
4 oz (100 g) desiccated coconut
3 oz (75 g) white sugar
pinch of salt
oil for shallow-frying
lemon juice

Pre-heat the oven to 325° F (180° C, gas mark 3). Combine all the
ingredients and beat into a smooth batter. Wipe a small frying
pan (6–7 in/15–18 cm) with a little oil and place over a moderate
heat. Spoon in just enough batter to cover the bottom of the pan.
Lightly brown one side of the pancake, then turn it over and
repeat on the other side. Roll up the pancake and place on a warm
plate in the moderate oven. Repeat for all the batter. Serve
sprinkled with lemon juice.

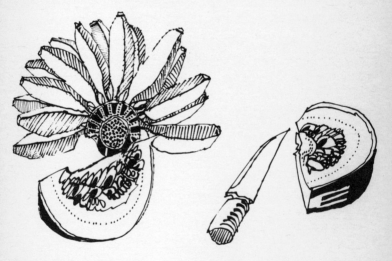

Deep-Fried Bananas   *Serves 4*

5 fl oz (150 ml) water
5 oz (150 g) rice flour *or* plain white flour
1 egg, beaten
2 tablespoons desiccated coconut
pinch of salt

4 firm bananas, peeled, sliced lengthwise and then crosswise
  to give 4 pieces per banana
oil for deep-frying

Combine the water, flour, egg, coconut and salt in a mixing bowl
and whisk into a smooth batter. Heat the oil for deep-frying until
it just starts to smoke. Dip the banana slices in the batter and fry
them 5 or 6 at a time until golden brown and crisp. Remove them
with a slotted spoon and drain on a paper towel before serving.
Repeat for all the banana pieces.

Bananas in Coconut Milk   *Serves 4*

4 firm bananas, peeled, sliced lengthwise and then crosswise
  to give 4 pieces per banana
12 fl oz (350 ml) medium coconut milk
2 tablespoons white sugar
½ teaspoon salt

Combine all the ingredients in a pan and bring to the boil. Reduce
the heat and simmer, uncovered, for 3–4 minutes. Remove from
the heat. Serve at room temperature or chilled.

Baked Ginger and Citrus Bananas   *Serves 6*

This dessert is more South-East Asian than characteristically
Thai. However, it is particularly good and lends itself well to
Western tastes and the Western kitchen.

2 oz (50 g) butter
2 oz (50 g) white sugar
1 tablespoon (15 ml) lemon juice
1 tablespoon (15 ml) orange juice
½ teaspoon powdered cinnamon
1 teaspoon grated lemon rind
2 teaspoons finely chopped ginger root
6 bananas, peeled and cut in half crosswise

Pre-heat the oven to 375°F (190°C, gas mark 5). Beat together
the butter and sugar and then beat in the remaining ingredients
except the bananas. Lightly grease a shallow baking dish and
arrange the banana pieces on the bottom. Pour over them the
butter and ginger mixture, and bake for 15 minutes. Serve
immediately.

Weights and Measures

The following conversion table gives the imperial and metric equivalents used in the recipes.

Weights		Liquids	
Imperial	Approximate metric equivalent	Imperial	Approximate metric equivalent
½ oz	15 g	¼ teaspoon	1.25 ml
1 oz	25 g	½ teaspoon	2.5 ml
2 oz	50 g	1 teaspoon	5 ml
3 oz	75 g	2 teaspoons	10 ml
4 oz	100 g	1 tablespoon	15 ml
5 oz	150 g	2 tablespoons	30 ml
6 oz	175 g	3 tablespoons	45 ml
7 oz	200 g		
8 oz	225 g	1 fl oz	25 ml
9 oz	250 g	2 fl oz	50 ml
10 oz	275 g	3 fl oz	75 ml
11 oz	300 g	4 fl oz	100 ml
12 oz	350 g	5 fl oz (¼ pint)	150 ml
13 oz	375 g	6 fl oz	175 ml
14 oz	400 g	7 fl oz	200 ml
15 oz	425 g	8 fl oz	225 ml
1 lb	450 g	9 fl oz	250 ml
2 lb	900 g	10 fl oz (½ pint)	275 ml
3 lb	1.4 kg	15 fl oz (¾ pint)	450 ml
		20 fl oz (1 pint)	550 ml

Exact Conversion 1 oz = 28.35 g

Index

Chicken *cont.*
  Whole – Simmered in Spiced
    Coconut Milk, 104
  with Basil and Chilli, 103
  Won-Ton, 108–9
Chillies, 10, 11, 15–16, 18–19, 25
  Beef and – Salad, 66
  Beef with – and Chinese
    Mushrooms, 75
  Chicken with Basil and, 103
  Pickled, 63
  Sauce, 88
Coconut, 10, 19–21, 126
  Baked – Custard, 130–1
  Cream, 19, 21
  Grapefruit and – Salad, 68
  Pancakes, 132
  Sauce, Cooked Vegetable Salad
    in, 64–5; Chicken in, 108
Coconut Milk, 19–21
  Bananas in, 133
  Beef in (*Rama bathing*), 78
  Soup, Lemon, Chicken and –,
    34–5
  Spiced, Whole Chicken
    Simmered in, 104
Coriander, 10, 11, 22
  Marinated – Fried Chicken,
    106–7
Crab Meat, Sautéd and Greens, 46
Crabs, Deep-Fried Stuffed, 95
Cream, sour, 19
Cucumber
  Boats with Beef Cargo, 70
  Relish, 64
  Salad, 64
  Sauce, 77, 89, 124
Curry, 9, 112–20
  Beef, 118–19; Green, 116–17,
    Massaman (*Thai Muslim*), 115
  Chicken, 118–19
  Fish and Vegetable, 120
  Noodles, Fried, 120
  Paste, 112–15; Green, 114;
    Massaman, 112–13; Mild, 115;
    Orange, 114; Red, 113
  Pork with Vegetables, 116
  Prawn, 117; – and Aubergine,
    94–5
  Rice, Fried, 119
  Sauce, 92–3
  Shrimp, 117

Desserts, 130–3 *see also individual
  entries*
Drinks, 9

Eggs, Son-in-law, 43
Equipment, 12

Fish, 9, 85–97, 103
  and Vegetable Curry, 120
  Cakes, Thai, 89
  Fermented (*Pla Ra*), 85
  Fiery – Salad, 69
  Fried, 87–9, 97; Fillet in Lemon
    Sauce, 91, with Chinese
    Mushrooms, 92; with Curry
    Sauce, 92–3
  Sauce (*Nam Pla*), 10, 22; Hot
    (*Nam Prik*), 122; Sweet and
    Hot, 124; Sweet and Sour, 88;
    Vietnamese, 123
  Simmered in Red Sauce, 94
  Soup, Fishball and Mushroom,
    32–3
  with Basil and Chilli, 103
Fruit, 9, 127–33 *see also individual
  entries*

Galangal, 22
Galloping Horses, 38–9
Garlic, 10, 11
Garnishes, 11–12
Ginger, 10, 22–3
  Baked – and Citrus Bananas, 133
  Lemon and – Fried Chicken and
    Mushrooms, 102–3
Grapefruit and Coconut Salads, 68

Hamburgers, Thai, 77

Lemon juice/rind, 10, 11, 24
  and Ginger Fried Chicken and
    Mushrooms, 102–3
  Soup, – Chicken and Coconut
    Milk, 34–5
  Sauce, 91
Lemon Grass, 23, 36
Limes, 11

Mackerel, Grilled with Hot Sauce,
  96
Mangoes, 127–9
  with Sticky Rice, 131

Index